Being a vampire doesn't make me an evil person. I would never intentionally hurt another individual to get blood, or for any other reason as a matter of fact.

Rather, I have found donors who let me take blood from them in a number of ways. When they don't wish to be bitten by me, I use a sterile lancet. Only a few drops come out from such a small wound, but it's enough to satisfy me, and it spares them a lot of pain.

We vampires are not necessarily bad people, and I would like others to know that. You may print this letter for that reason.

—Vampiress Paulina

About the Author

Konstantinos was born on Long Island, New York, where he currently resides. He has a bachelor's degree in English and technical writing, and is the author of several articles. This is his second book for Llewellyn.

Konstantinos has been researching the occult and practicing Western Magick for almost a decade. Through his lectures at colleges and bookstores in the New York area, the author has helped several victims of psychic-vampire attack.

When not writing or pursuing his occult interests, Konstantinos enjoys listening to music and reading. He is also the vocalist of the Gothic band Bell, Book & Candle.

To Write to the Author

If you wish to contact the author or would like more information about this book, please write to the author in care of Llewellyn Worldwide, and we will forward your request. Both the author and publisher appreciate hearing from you and learning of your enjoyment of this book. Llewellyn Worldwide cannot guarantee that every letter written to the author will be answered, but all will be forwarded. Please write to:

Konstantinos
℅ Llewellyn Worldwide
P.O. Box 64383, Dept. K380-8,
St. Paul, MN 55164-0383, U.S.A.

Please enclose a self-addressed stamped envelope for reply, or $1.00 to cover costs. If outside U.S.A., enclose international postal reply coupon.

Vampires

The Occult Truth

Konstantinos

2002
Llewellyn Publications
St. Paul, MN 55164-0383, USA

FIRST EDITION
Ninth printing, 2002

Cover design: Tom Grewe
Book design, layout, and editing: Jessica Thoreson
Author photo: Michele

Cataloging-in-Publication Data
Konstantinos, 1972—
    Vampires: the occult truth / Konstantinos. -- 1st. ed.
      p.   cm.
    Includes bibliographical references and index.
    ISBN 1-56718-380-8 (trade pbk.)
    1. Vampires. I. Title.
  BF1556.K66   1996
  133.4'23--dc20   96-12238
                                         CIP

Llewellyn Worldwide does not participate in, endorse, or have any authority or responsibility concerning private business transactions between our authors and the public.
  All mail addressed to the author is forwarded but the publisher cannot, unless specifically instructed by the author, give out an address or phone number.

Llewellyn Publications
A Division of Llewellyn Worldwide, Ltd.
P.O. Box 64383, Dept. 1-56718-380-8
St. Paul, MN 55164-0383
www.llewellyn.com

Printed in the United States of America

Other Books by Konstantinos

Summoning Spirits: The Art of Magical Evocation
Contact the Other Side: Seven Methods of
Afterlife Communication
Nocturnal Witchcraft

Forthcoming Books by Konstantinos

Gothic Grimoire

Dedication

For Michele, my true love and soul-mate.

Acknowledgements

The following people deserve a special thanks for helping me make this book possible:

My parents, for many years of support and understanding.

Michele, for putting up with a lot of strangeness.

Carl Weschcke, for making it all happen like magic.

Nancy Mostad, for priceless guidance and friendship.

Jessica Thoreson, for being a great editor.

Dave Vanian, Andrew Eldritch, and Peter Murphy, for hours of entertainment.

Anne Rice, Tanith Lee, and Poppy Z. Brite, for prose of inspiration.

And to all the vampires, living and undead, who lent me their stories....

Table of Contents

Introduction

It is 3:00 A.M. Still uncertain why she woke up, the girl tries to roll over and go back to sleep. But she can't. She's paralyzed. The room seems too quiet; in fact, if not for the familiar surroundings, the startled sleeper would swear that she was somewhere else. Terror fills her, along with the feeling that something is coming.

Out in the hall, strange hollow footsteps sound, and become louder—she starts to feel dizzy. Closer, closer, then the sound stops; whatever is in the hall is now right outside the door.

At the foot of the bed, a dark figure seems to appear out of thin air. Like a mist it comes over her. It is heavy, so heavy— it crushes. Her chest has a hard time rising and falling to keep up with the increasing beat of her heart.

She wants to scream, but nothing comes out. Two red, blazing eyes are all that pierce the darkness of the mass above her. Weight, suffocation, then falling....

In an instant, the feeling ends and the girl springs up. Everything seems normal again, yet she feels so tired. Weakness pulls her back to her pillow; somehow, she manages to fall asleep again.

"There are such beings as vampires...."

With those words, Dr. Van Helsing, in the novel *Dracula*, began his lecture on the powers of the undead. Of course, books like *Dracula* are fiction, right?

Well, that novel is, and even though Vlad Dracula was a real man, there is no evidence to support that he ever became an undead creature of the night. However, there are real vampires, though they might not always take the form that most people expect.

In the pages that follow, we'll take a look at the different types of vampires found in the world, and explore the hidden, or occult, truth behind each. So, curl up in your favorite spot, and prepare to learn the facts about what most believe to be only fiction....

Chapter One

Separating Fact from Fiction

While preparing this book, I have been asked, by many skeptical people, questions like: "How could vampires really exist?" or even, "Are you serious?" Most went on to add that the bloodsuckers of fiction seem a bit hard to believe in; after all, if they really feed on humans like they are portrayed in the movies as doing, wouldn't there be an enormous number of victims found in alleys, or perhaps even in graveyards, on any given morning? There obviously haven't been any such victims, though, because their blood-drained bodies and the familiar puncture wounds on their necks would have attracted enough media attention to make belief in vampires commonplace by now.

These types of arguments make it a little hard for most people in the twentieth century to believe in the existence of an order of being that can live forever and feed off the vitality of humans. In this technological age, who among us finds it easy to accept that such a creature can escape the notice of science?

Before we get into the hard-to-believe nature of the vampire's attributes and abilities, let's do away with the need for any pre-existing scientific skepticism. I consider those who are interested in the occult to be the scientists of the future. If everyone were to accept that what science has not yet discovered does not exist, science would stagnate and society could not advance. Keep in mind that a lot of things that the ancients considered mystical have been explained by science—and the ancients believed in vampires.

Let's apply some rational, scientific thinking to the subject of this book's study. The truths presented in these pages have been proven empirically, both by myself and by others before me. In each case presented in the chapters that follow, all the evidence (which takes many different forms) is presented fully to show how certain conclusions were drawn. In other words, don't take my word for the bizarre, yet true, facts you are about to read. Please judge them for yourself. My intention in writing this book was not to create a fantastic tale of vampirism and expect others to believe it; that is what vampire novels are for (and there are a lot of those—around the time of this writing, two or three are published every month, with even more coming out near Halloween). Instead, I wanted to present the first complete treatise on the subject—one that looks at all the realities of vampirism in detail and separates the truth from the fiction.

Doing away with preconceived notions is one of the hardest things that an investigator of the paranormal has to do. It is important to keep an open mind when dealing with things that do not lend themselves to easy observation—to my knowledge, no immortal vampire has ever knocked on a medical scientist's door and asked for a physical exam. The subject of our study is a covert one, and we therefore have to look for covert clues. Solving the puzzle of vampirism requires that we see all the pieces and recognize them for what they are. Not keeping an open mind makes that impossible.

In the case of vampires, we have to remember that they are not fictional creatures created by early novelists. The undead are creatures of folklore, and the first literature mentioning them was in every way considered nonfiction by those who penned it; in fact, most of those early treatises were written by the respected scholars of the day. However, few people are aware of the various tales of the undead that were not "made up" for the racks of bookstores, but were instead documented for preservation in the libraries of the time.

Fortunately, age-old occult literature about vampires still exists. From various first-hand accounts, diaries, and investigations, one can quickly see that something very real was being described. However, there are several distinctions between the vampires described in those texts and the beings portrayed in popular fiction and movies. Before looking for the reality behind the legends, it is important to first separate the legends from the fiction. Writers like Anne Rice, Bram Stoker, Tanith Lee, and Brian Lumley, among countless others, have created fantastic attributes and powers for their vampires, but those beings are not the subject of our study. Trying to find the truth behind those fictional creations is as ridiculous as trying to find the truth behind the monster created by Mary Shelley in *Frankenstein*.

Therefore, let's begin our uncovering of the truth by defining the attributes of the vampire of folklore—the creature that you might be surprised to discover exists in more than one form.

The Appearance of the Vampire

The vampire of folklore does not closely match the romantic character that has been developed in the past century. Since Bela Lugosi's suave portrayal of Dracula in 1931, vampires in fiction have become progressively better looking and more and more associated with sexuality through the years—a far cry from the creatures of folklore.

What does the vampire of folklore look like? Ancient descriptions of the appearance of the undead vary just enough to indicate that two distinct types of beings were described: vampires that seemed for the most part to be physical, and vampires that had almost phantom-like attributes. Of the two, the first type of creature was reported the least often. As we'll see later in the book, several physical cases of vampirism have been dismissed by modern-day medical experts as having natural causes. For now, let's deal with each in turn, starting with the first.

The typical "physical" vampire or revenant of Europe did not wear a cape or stylish clothing. Remember, the undead are supposed to be the risen dead. They therefore appear, according to folklore, as most corpses would if they were dragged out of the ground. In other words, when people reported seeing vampires hundreds of years ago, they described them as wearing what they were buried in—a shroud.

The descriptions would go on to include a few pronounced characteristics: For starters, the physical vampire of folklore was not pale. In fact, most documents indicate that the skin color of an undead typically had a reddish tinge, as if the blood it ingested infused every cell of its body. That made a lot of sense to the investigators of the time, because when they would drive a stake through a suspected vampire's heart, blood would explode out of the hole as if the body were saturated with it.

That brings us to the next characteristic of physical vampires. Unlike the thin, almost emaciated look that vampires have in movies, the folkloric creature was often reported as appearing bloated. Again, that seemed perfectly logical to the vampire hunters of the time. They believed that the bloated appearance was a result of the vampire being gorged with blood.

Other characteristics of the physical folkloric vampire are ones that have been used by various authors of fiction. Those attributes include a horrible odor or rancid breath; long fingernails and hair, which, according to folklore, keep growing in a vampire; sharp teeth, although not necessarily eye-teeth fangs; and in some cases, eyes that blaze with a supernatural, often red, light.

Keep in mind that many of the above characteristics were for the most part observed in vampires that were in their coffins. A lot of the cases of physical vampirism were "solved" when a vampire hunter would open the coffin of an alleged undead and dispose of it with a wooden stake and, usually, fire. Often, the characteristics of natural decomposition would be confused for undeath. For that reason, as we will deal with in Chapter Three, several famous documented cases of physical vampirism involve vampires that cannot be proven as such.

The other type of vampire encountered in folklore is the one that possesses phantom-like attributes. That creature is found in some of the most famous cases of vampirism, including that of Peter Plogojowitz, which will be described later in this book. As we'll see below, what is most interesting about that type of creature is that it seems to be a vampiric spirit that is connected in some ways to the corpse it once animated.

The phantom-like vampire of folklore feeds on living people while they are in bed at night. When the vampire appears, its features are usually quite familiar to the villagers it attacks—they recognize it as being one of their deceased neighbors. We will not examine the sort of attack made by the phantom-like type of vampire at this point (although the short scene in the Introduction is an example). Suffice it to say that once the creature removes itself, the victim usually recalls the identity of the specter, often inciting a frenzy in the villagers.

The actual appearance of the phantom-like vampire, other than resembling the deceased person who became undead, varies in different accounts. Often, the vampire is described as assuming a dark form, with its facial features becoming clear for only a moment before the actual attack begins. Other accounts indicate that the vampire, although somewhat transparent, was immediately recognized by the victim when it entered his or her bedroom at night.

Even though the preceding descriptions are almost universal among the cases of folkloric vampirism, the more recent and even modern-day incidents of spectral, vampiric attack indicate that victims only rarely recognize their phantom assailants. For the most part, vampires of the above type are described as dark masses, with occasional reported observations of red or glowing eyes. The fact that fewer eyewitnesses of the above type of creature in the past hundred years notice any facial features indicates that there is a severe shift in popular beliefs. In other words, fewer people today believe that the dead can rise to harm the living. In the past, however, the belief was strong and could possibly be the reason that a supernatural assailant would quickly assume the features of the deceased.

Whether or not the villagers of the past were right in their assumptions of the identities of phantom vampires cannot be proven. What they found when they opened the graves of those that were identified as the undead is still interesting. The appearance of the physical vampire described earlier is in many ways similar to the corpses of the spectral vampire as well. Suspected bodies, when exhumed, often appeared bloated, ruddy, and somewhat fresh, even months after burial.

If the vampire we are discussing is truly a phantom, why should its corpse appear in that bizarre way? As we shall see later, the physical attributes described by the vampire hunters of years ago can be explained naturally. For example, when a body decomposes, gases are created within it, causing the body to expand and appear bloated. But what if the instincts of those hunters were stronger than their abilities at conveying their feelings in words?

The general occult theory on the spectral type of vampire that thrived in folklore is that the spirit fed on either blood or energy (or both) by night, and by day returned to the corpse to infuse it with this energy. That would explain how a vampire could come up from its coffin without disturbing the soil—it could simply move through the ground in its astral body. Why a spectral vampire would wish to remain in its earthly form by day is another matter. Later in the book we'll take a look at several occult theories explaining the above process.

Powers of the Vampire

As we've discussed, the difference between folklore and fiction is unclear to most when describing the appearance of the vampire. The same holds true when identifying the powers of the vampire; misconceptions abound. Again we have the problem: what's documented and what's made up? Before going any further, let's briefly clear that up to some extent. Later, in the chapters that deal with each of the different types of vampires, we will go into great detail when describing their powers, along with an in-depth look at instances when those powers were displayed.

The physical vampire of folklore was not as endowed with supernatural abilities as its fictional counterparts are. In fact, most documented cases indicate that those vampires did little more than come in through windows, suck the blood of their victims, and flee into the night once again. Of course, the powers of a folkloric vampire depend on its ethnic species.

Yes, you read correctly; that last phrase is "ethnic species." I use this to indicate that each culture had different names and attributes for vampires. When vampires are separated into two classes (as we have been doing in this chapter), something interesting happens. The primary powers of the vampires from different countries that fit into the same groups (physical or phantom-like) are found to be almost identical. By "primary powers," I refer to the means vampires use to obtain their sustenance. Conversely, the differences between the secondary powers of ethnic vampire species are in certain cases extreme. For the purposes of this book, "secondary powers" are any abilities that vampires do not need to obtain sustenance; keep in mind that those powers still might serve some other purposes that aid survival.

Later, we'll divide vampires into four groups to further identify their powers, but for now, let's get to some examples of the distinctions in types of powers. It will probably come as no great surprise to anyone that one of the primary powers of the physical vampire is the ability to live off the blood of humans. Another primary power is also one that most people have come to expect from the undead—great strength. In most cases of physical vampire attack, the victim is reported as being unable to wrestle off the vampire while it feeds.

The secondary powers of the physical vampire vary to a great extent. Throughout this book, you will come across several secondary powers exhibited by vampires in different cases. However, to whet your appetite for now, here are a couple of the least-known, and most unusual, secondary powers that are found in different types of physical vampires.

For starters, in a few countries there is a belief that vampires can still have sexual relations with the living. Unlike what popular fiction promotes, that was not considered a desirable thing. The vampire's power to do that is similar to the powers of the incubus or succubus. Any children of such a union are born with the ability to sense the presence of an undead. Also, those offspring are considered (by many cultures) to be able to destroy vampires with ease.

Another attribute of the physical vampire (in some areas) is its ability to at some point live life again as a mortal. Of particular note is the *langsuir,* a female vampire of Malaysia which can be captured and cured of her curse in such a way that she can once again live an almost normal life. The *langsuir,* along with several other species of vampires, will be discussed in more detail in the next chapter.

The primary powers of the phantom-like undead are not as widely known. The two that always seem to be present in documented cases (both ancient and new) are the ability to drain vitality from living humans (not necessarily blood—most likely just energy), and the ability to cause paralysis in their victims. As shown later on, the taking of vitality is almost always done in the form of psychic energy.

Sometimes, it was suspected that such a vampire could still take blood in an immaterial form, because the victim would on occasion have bite marks or scratches on his or her body. However, modern occult theory has a different explanation for those marks. That's dealt with in Chapter Seven. Phantom-like vampires have some interesting secondary powers as well.

Many phantom-like vampires display shape-changing ability. Numerous victims who have survived this type of vampire's attack report the changing of the creature's form as it prepares to attack, and sometimes, during the attack itself. This power is not limited to the appearance of the vampire; it seems that the creature can also change from immaterial to material form, and vice versa, at will. That would appear to make things difficult for the would-be vampire hunter.

Another interesting secondary power of the spectral vampire is its ability to fly or levitate. That seems easy to believe for a creature that can assume a non-corporeal form. In most documents detailing the attack of one of those creatures, the creatures are described as hovering over their victims before lowering themselves as heavy masses upon their prey. Also, the phantom vampires are reported as flying away almost instantaneously when they are finished feeding. Of course, they are able to fly through walls and the like.

The Four Types of Vampires

Now that we've become comfortable with the distinctions between physical and phantom-like vampires, it's time to shake things up a little bit. Let's divide those groups again. First, let's agree that all vampires do have something in common.

If you look in a dictionary you will find a few definitions that relate to vampires. The definition of vampirism itself is interesting because it is often given as "the practice of preying upon others," or something similar. Does that necessarily have to mean preying on the blood of others? Some dictionaries go on to make that distinction, but we shall not in this book. Vampires, in reality, are those creatures who prey upon others for sustenance. The source of that sustenance, the method of obtaining it, and the need it fulfills are what distinguish the different types of vampires from each other.

Immortal Blood Drinkers

For the most part, immortal blood drinkers are the creatures we have been describing so far as "physical vampires." These vampires are the ones that are most similar to the undead found in popular fiction, although, of the several ethnic species in this category, no one particular type possesses even half the powers attributed by authors and screenwriters to their vampires. With that distinction made, the existence of immortal blood drinkers should seem more feasible, but as we shall see in Chapter Three, although there is a lot of evidence that seemingly supports the existence of this type of being, a lot of it is not completely convincing. For that reason, many who read this book might feel that immortal blood drinkers are the least likely type of vampire to exist. However, before you make up your mind, take into consideration the fact that their existence cannot be entirely disproved.

Mortal Blood Drinkers

Since the beginning of recorded history, common mortals have felt the need to drink blood for a variety of reasons. Those reasons range from ancient cultures' beliefs in the power of blood, especially the blood of an enemy; to a particular form of insanity, Renfield's Syndrome, which is named after the character in *Dracula* who is a zoophagous (life-eater). In Chapter Four we will look briefly at those who drank blood in the past but were not necessarily undead. However, the main focus of Chapter Five will be on the living blood drinkers who are active today. As a result of a few ads that I placed (again, see Chapter Five), I received from these modern-day creatures of the night an astounding eighty-two letters! Of course I can't include all of them in this book, but I have chosen a few that provide insight to the lives and beliefs of these living vampires.

Unintentional Psychic Vampires

This is a type of vampire that most never find out about, including the vampires themselves! Unintentional psychic vampires are people who feed on the psychic energy of others unconsciously. The reasons their bodies do so vary from case to case, but for the most part, they "feed" because they need the extra energy to survive some illness. Occult explanations of how that occurs, and how it can be stopped, are included in Chapters Eight and Ten, respectively. Vampires of this type are often much older than their victims because, unfortunately, illnesses often set in as one ages. Those illnesses usually deplete a person to the point where his or her body feeds off younger individuals to remain vital. However, the unintentional psychic vampire can just as easily be a child, or within any other age group. The fact that vampires of this type feed without a victim's knowledge of their doing so makes them dangerous.

Intentional Psychic Vampires

Of the four types of vampires, the intentional psychic vampires are the ones that should be feared most. That is for two reasons: they cannot be destroyed or thwarted by any physical means (i.e., a wooden stake or a cross), and as two surveys show, about one out of five people are attacked by a vampire of this type during the course of their lives. Luckily, those attacks are rarely fatal. Intentional psychic vampires usually start out as individuals who drain others of psychic energy on purpose (occasionally under some kind of group guidance, as discussed in Chapter Nine). When they master that, they move on to astrally projecting and feeding off the energy of sleeping victims. Eventually, like all of us do, those individuals die. At that time, they become earthbound entities that need to continue feeding in the previously described manner to survive; they use the psychic energy they absorb to keep their own astral bodies from decaying. We'll get into the details of how and why that occurs in Chapter Nine.

What will become more evident as we proceed is that certain vampire types have more evidence supporting their existence than others. I have hinted at the amount of that evidence available so far, but you should be the judge of what that all means.

Intermingled with the chapters in this book that deal with each of the preceding vampire groups, are some chapters that deal with some of the occult theories of vampirism. First of all, the next chapter will deal with some of the ancient beliefs and theories that attempted to explain vampires. Also in Chapter Two is an explanation of several ethnic species of vampires, some of which we have hinted at so far.

In addition to the descriptive chapters are two that should be of considerable interest to anyone who wishes to protect him or herself from a vampire's attack. The first of those, Chapter Six, explains various methods taken from folklore for keeping oneself safe from immortal blood drinkers. That chapter also contains some safety suggestions to keep in mind if you run into (or are) a mortal blood drinker. As you might guess, AIDS and other diseases make that type of vampirism just as dangerous as any other.

The second chapter to deal with protection from vampirism, Chapter Ten, deals with methods for preventing the attack of psychic vampires. If you recall, I mentioned earlier that intentional psychic vampires are dangerous because they cannot be thwarted by any physical means. For that reason, Chapter Ten will deal with non-physical methods for protecting oneself from psychic attacks. Those are simple "rituals" that anyone can perform, and which will definitely work.

This book clearly contains a great deal more than just a collection of interesting bits of folklore. Even though a lot of the information in it is age-old, a lot of it is also new. In fact, some of the modern cases of psychic vampirism described in Chapters Eight and Nine are ones I have personally investigated. Furthermore, I have included in Chapter Three an account of an immortal blood drinker that terrorized a Greek village in the early 1900s. The true story was told to me by a witness' daughter, who now lives in America.

When reading the descriptions of the vampires in each of the true cases presented in this book, try to identify the primary and secondary powers and abilities of each type of vampire. That should help you make up your own mind as to whether or not there are enough similarities between the creatures to warrant their existence.

Before we can deal with modern instances of vampirism, we have to look first at the ancient ones. Let's start our analysis of the occult truth behind vampires by going back in time a bit to the first vampire legends.

About five thousand years back, that is....

Chapter Two

Vampire Beliefs
from Around the World

Mesopotamia is often referred to as the "cradle of civilization" because it fostered what is most likely the world's first organized nation, Sumer (not to mention the several civilizations that followed). From the valley between the Tigris and Euphrates rivers has come the world's first epic tales, laws, methods of writing, agricultural techniques, metallurgical advances, and beliefs in the undead.

We are mostly interested in that last "first." In this chapter, we will explore a great many ancient beliefs in the undead, starting with Sumer, then moving forward in time to selected areas around the world to look at what other cultures from other times thought about vampires.

Why examine the ancient beliefs at all? Primarily because experience has shown the occult researchers of the world that ancient theories often have a lot more than just a grain of truth to them. Even though their observations were distorted at times, the first scribes of vampire lore have provided modern-day vampire researchers with a lot of "hints" that have made uncovering the truth about the creatures of the night possible.

Notice that the following sections of vampire lore are divided by culture or geographic location rather than by time. That was done so that the beliefs of each individual civilization could be examined from past to present without interruption. Also included within each section are descriptions of the different types of vampires believed in by each culture throughout the ages (the number of species described in each section varies, as some cultures believed in more types of vampires than did others).

Several of those species could actually be the same creatures. Each culture might have just called them by different names and, in several cases, might have noticed only some of the vampires' traits. When reading the descriptions of those vampires, remember to look for the similarities between them (as explained in the last chapter) that put them into one of the categories already discussed.

Before we begin our series of brief looks at the ancient vampire beliefs of the world, let's clear something up right now. A few vampire researchers have declared that the Indus River Valley civilization, which thrived at around the same time as that of the Sumerians, is actually the birthplace of the vampire myth. That might be true; however, the evidence suggests that they believed in a vampire deity rather than in a race of creatures. For that reason, we will refer to the Mesopotamians as the first to believe in undead creatures. Of course, we'll take a look at the beliefs of the Indus Valley inhabitants later as well.

With that said, let's go back to the roots of the vampire legend. Because of its importance, the section on Sumer that follows is slightly longer than the ones that come after it.

Mesopotamia and Modern Iraq

The first nation to inhabit the fertile crescent of Mesopotamia was Sumer. Although it's not entirely clear when the civilization first appeared in the area (some say it was about 4000 B.C.E.), the following facts are certain: by the year 3100 B.C.E., their culture was already highly developed, the earliest archaeologically proven dynasty had begun, the first cities were built, and city and state religions were set up and practiced.

However, despite all of their achievements, some of which were listed in the beginning of this chapter, they were obviously not as technologically advanced as us, which makes it far too easy for us in the twentieth century to laugh at their ideas. That is unfortunate, because the Sumerians' lack of technological advancement is what made them more open-minded than most of us are today. In fact, they dismissed no phenomena without first attempting to explain it in some way. Of course, they might not always have been right in their assumptions, but as analysis has shown, many of their hypotheses have stood the test of time.

A perfect example of the insight of the Sumerians is found in their system of mathematics. Even though they used a sexagesimal (base 60) system, as opposed to our base 100 system, the Sumerians still had a vast knowledge of geometry and were able to use their mathematical systems to calculate the necessary dimensions for several impressive pieces of architecture. If the Sumerians were able to create correct mathematical theorems using a different system of thought, then they might also have been right about other things, like their beliefs in vampires.

For various reasons discussed in the last chapter, immortal blood drinkers and intentional psychic vampires are probably the two most vicious types of creatures. The Sumerians managed to find room for both of those dark beings in their belief system. To get an idea of just how seriously they took the notion of the existence of vampires, all one has to do is look at a major precaution taken at the time against the undead. That is, the priests and priestesses in Sumer were trained to deal with both types of creatures because the citizens felt a real need for protection (similar to the way that citizens today demand more police protection).

To the Sumerians, evil was a very real force in the world. The belief in demons, and even in dark gods, was common at the time, so it is understandable that they would accept the existence of vampires. Wouldn't that belief have to come from somewhere? What did the Sumerians witness to cause them to explain the nature of the undead in their literature? Perhaps we'll never know the cause; we can only view the results.

Now that we've established, to some degree, that the Sumerians believed in vampires, let's examine some of the major species of vampire found in the area.

The most well-documented vampire-like creature from Sumer is the *ekimmu*. Like many vampires of folklore, it was believed that an *ekimmu* was created when someone died a violent death or was not buried properly. While not overtly called vampires, the descriptions given make them appear as real, intentional psychic vampires, nonetheless. That is because they were considered demonic, phantom-like entities that roamed the earth, unable to rest, in search of victims. In the excellent book *The Devils and Evil Spirits of Babylonia*, by R. Campbell Thompson, the attack pattern of the creatures is described. Thompson explains that when an *ekimmu* found a helpless individual, the creature would seize the victim and torment him or her until a priest or priestess could come and perform a ritual or exorcism to force the vampire off.

Blood is not mentioned in connection with the creature, but descriptions of the *ekimmu* often include mentions of "evil wind gusts" that seem to be metaphors for its psychic nature.

This is important because, in Sumerian mythology, wind is often shown as a manifestation of psychic or magical power. For example, with a breath, the Babylonian god Marduk gave life to the first man. In fact, as we shall see later, breath and the transfer of psychic energy are closely related.

Another creature from Mesopotamia that fits the role of an undead is the *uruku* or *utukku* (I have seen it spelled both ways). In fact, the *uruku* is actually referred to in a cuneiform inscription as a "vampyre which attacks man." Unfortunately, not as much is known about the *uruku* as is known about the *ekimmu*, but the fact that it was called a "vampyre" warrants its inclusion here.

The next race of vampiric entity is one that was very feared: the Seven Demons. These beings have been mentioned in numerous Mesopotamian religious texts and incantations, like the following excerpt of a Sumerian banishment (taken from Thompson's previously mentioned book):

Demons that have no shame,
Seven are they!
Knowing no care...
Knowing no mercy,
They rage against mankind:
They spill their blood like rain,
Devouring their flesh [and] sucking their veins.
Where the images of the gods are, there they quake...
They are demons full of violence
Ceaselessly devouring blood.
Invoke the ban against them,
That they no more return to this neighborhood...

The creatures described in the above banishment clearly have some of the attributes ascribed to immortal blood-drinking vampires. The blood drinking and vein sucking described in the incantation are not the only interesting attributes mentioned, however. The eighth line in the excerpt indicates that the creatures are afraid of the images of the gods of Sumer, or of where those images are kept—in temples. This belief had its parallel in the past few centuries when it was accepted that a vampire could not bear to enter a church.

Before going forward in time a bit, let's take a look at a specific entity that has been called a vampire by many modern researchers (although there doesn't seem to be much evidence to support the fact). That Sumerian entity is the female demon Lilith. Her first "appearance" was in the myth of Inanna and the *hullupu* tree. In that legend, Lilith is called a "dark maid" who lives in the trunk of the *hullupu* tree (a tree that the goddess Inanna wanted to use to make her throne) and is little more than a nuisance to the goddess.

Since the myth's introduction, Lilith was viewed as a creature of evil, cast out by the gods. This outcast status should sound a bit familiar to anyone who's been exposed to at least some form of modern vampire fiction. However, the first appearance of Lilith was definitely not vampiric. She would later be considered a succubus (a female demon that has sexual relations with men and drains them of energy) by other cultures (particularly the Hebrews), but as far as the people of Mesopotamia were concerned, Lilith was not a vampire.

Keep in mind that none of the preceding vampire species was ever reported in a manner that resembles modern journalism. There is no mention anywhere in the tablets that survived the Mesopotamian culture of a dated sighting of a vampire in any form. Rather, documents have been uncovered that indicate people accepted their existence as fact. As to what evidence supported the vampires' existence, we'll probably never know.

After the decline of Sumer in the second millennium B.C.E., vampire lore in the general vicinity of Mesopotamia seemed to die out for a while. However, in more recent times (the fifteenth century), the area, now called Iraq, became rich in those beliefs once again. This time, the undead began to take on the guises of two different creatures: ghouls and vampires. Thanks to popular fiction (the great distorter of folklore), the classification of "ghoul" has become a bit ambiguous. In this book, the word "ghoul" will be used in reference to a creature that eats the remains of a dead body and, on occasion, the body or blood (or both) of a living person.

What's interesting about ghouls is that they can be living or dead creatures, and in at least one famous case, they can turn into vampires if killed. That well-known folktale (it is unclear if there is any factual basis for it) was eventually adapted and included in the complete *One Thousand and One Arabian Nights*. In the story, Abdul-Hassan, the son of a wealthy Baghdad merchant, was supposed to marry a woman his father had chosen for him. Instead, he fell in love with a different woman, Nadilla, the daughter of a sage. After some pleading on the part of Abdul-Hassan, his father agreed to let his son marry Nadilla.

The newlywed husband soon noticed that his wife never ate any food and that she left their bed every night, to return only at sunrise. One night, Abdul-Hassan decided to follow his wife and see just where it was she went every night. He lay in bed pretending to be asleep, and after Nadilla left, he followed her—to a graveyard. There he saw her feasting with a few other ghouls upon the flesh of long-buried bodies.

Abdul-Hassan quickly returned to bed, and the next day at supper, tried to get his wife to eat. She refused, and to that Abdul-Hassan responded that she was keeping her appetite for her feasts with the ghouls. Trembling, Nadilla left and went to bed. That night she rose and attacked her husband, tearing his throat; Nadilla then sucked his blood. Abdul-Hassan must have been ready for her, however, because he managed to strike her dead immediately.

Three days later, at midnight, she returned, apparently as a vampire, and tried once again to suck his blood, but Abdul-Hassan escaped her. The next day, he went to her tomb, burned Nadilla's body, and threw the ashes into the Tigris river.

That tale pretty much sums up the type of vampire lore found in Iraq in more recent times. (Creatures with ghoul-like attributes also appear in the folklore of the Orient, but their legends and tales are not directly mingled with those of vampire folklore. For that reason, ghouls as a type of creature will not be examined in any great detail in this book.)

Now, let's move to the lands east of Mesopotamia or modern Iraq: India and its surrounding countries.

India and Surrounding Countries

Just as civilization developed in the valley between the Tigris and Euphrates rivers, so did a civilization form in another fertile area some 1,500 miles away, in the Indus River Valley (Northern India). Although it is likely that the Mesopotamian culture predates that of the Indus tribes by a few centuries, there is some evidence that suggests the two cultures are related. In his book *The Sumerians,* archaeologist C. Leonard Woolley wrote that rectangular stamp seals found at both sites (Mesopotamia and the Indus Valley) bear a strong enough resemblance to indicate that the civilizations are in some way connected.

Whether or not that statement is true is not as important to this discussion as the fact that both cultures believed in vampire-like beings several millennia ago. In fact, the people of the Indus River Valley are also accorded with their own historical first: they were the first to believe in the concept of vampire gods. And, as we shall see later, there are some in the world today who still have the same "faith."

The vampire gods were ruthless, demonic beings that most people appeased out of fear alone. In the introduction to the novel *Varney the Vampire*, which is entitled "The Vampire in Legend, Lore, and Literature," Professor Devendra P. Varma describes paintings and carvings found in the Indus Valley. The pieces of art, which date back about five thousand years, depict hideous creatures with green faces and fangs. Those beings are believed to be the first vampire gods.

Nothing more is really known about the vampire gods of the Indus Valley. However, what is known is that the belief soon spread into the surrounding areas, and developed as the years passed. Specific gods with their own names and attributes began to appear. The first was the Nepalese Lord of Death. His fangs were not his only vampiric feature. He was also shown holding a skull full of blood (apparently for use as a cup from which he drank) and standing on top of a pile of human skeletons. The god seems to have taken his sustenance from blood and death.

Another vampire god with a similar title was the Tibetan Lord of Death. He had similar features to the vampire gods described earlier (a green face, fangs, etc.), and was considered a creature who lived off the blood of humans.

A more recently-worshiped vampire-like deity is Kali. She was worshiped by a bloodthirsty group known as the Thugee cult, whose members murdered tens of thousands until the 1800s, when the British Empire wiped them out. The Thugs would often drain their victims of blood and roast the remains on spits before the statue of their goddess. Why blood sacrifice was used is pretty clear. One myth states that Kali battled a demon named Raktavija, and every time a single drop of his blood was shed, a thousand new demons appeared to face the goddess. Kali drank his blood to defeat him.

The traditional image of Kali could also be considered vampiric. She was often depicted as being completely covered in blood. Her mouth was sinister, and not only because she had fangs; she was often shown with her tongue sticking out—possibly to hint that she lapped up her blood sacrifices. Of course, the images of Kali included the assorted skulls that were found in the images of other vampire deities.

In addition to the mythology of vampire deities, beliefs in vampire-like creatures in India and surrounding areas developed over the years. Soon, the vampire gods were not alone. Following are some of the undead creatures from the area that never achieved a god-like status.

A particularly vicious species of vampire was the *raksashas* or *raksashis* (male and female, respectively). Those creatures were described as having fangs, five legs, and bodies soaked in blood. To add to their vampiric traits, the *raksashas* and *raksashis* supposedly lived in graveyards and have been described in many texts as "blood drinkers," although some etymologists argue that the name means "destroyers."

The *raksashas* and *raksashis* were first described in the Vedas (Hindu religious texts) in the second millennium B.C.E. It is believed that because of the Hindu acceptance of the existence of vampiric creatures, the beliefs were able to spread easily to other regions along with the religion.

An example of this spread is found to the east of the Indian Ocean in Malaysia, where the Hindus told of a vampire called the *langsuir*. Any woman giving birth who died upon discovering that her child was stillborn was thought to become one of those creatures. The *langsuir* was not described as having fangs like other vampires, rather, it supposedly had a hole in the back of its neck that it used to suck blood. If you recall, in the last chapter we discussed this creature's ability to once again live life as a mortal. That was supposedly accomplished by a mortal who would cut the vampire's nails and hair, and stuff them into the hole in her neck.

Before we move away from Malaysia, one more vampire (not a species, but an individual, legendary creature) deserves mention—the *penanggalan*. That creature was also believed to be female; a woman who was interrupted in the middle of a penance ceremony. From her great shock and rapid movement, her head became separated from her body and flew off as an evil spirit. The creature was later heard whining on the roofs of houses where children were being born. She apparently wished to get inside the houses to drink the children's blood.

Moving back a little closer to India, we come to the country of Tibet. As we have already seen, they had an early belief in a vampire god. They, too, developed vampire folklore that followed their religious beliefs. As in India, some vampire lore ended up in their religious texts, particularly *The Tibetan Book of the Dead*. In it, fifty-eight blood-drinking deities are described. Those Wrathful Deities, as they were called (actually, the description in *The Tibetan Book of the Dead* makes them seem more like entities than deities), inhabited the land of the dead. The Tibetans also believed that the spirits of the dead could inhabit corpses and cause them to rise and attack the living.

Other Indian vampires include the *vetalas*, which have appeared in various forms. Of particular interest is the old hag who sucks blood. As we shall see later, hags are associated with vampirism in other countries as well. The *bhuta* is another vampire-like being, or rather, a category of vampires. Those creatures were described in various ways, most notably as ghouls who eat the remains of humans, and as vampires who attack those who approach graveyards.

Finally, we come to three related beings. The first, the *hantu saburo*, is a being who commands dogs and uses them to hunt humans. When the animals catch the prey, the vampire feeds. The second is the *hantu dodong*, which resides in caves and lives off the blood of animals. Finally, the *hantu parl* looks for wounded individuals and drinks their blood when they are helpless to stop it.

Let's continue our investigation by traveling even further to the east.

China and the Pacific

Often considered a land of mystery to those in Europe, the Far East doesn't fail to meet those expectations with its vampire "mysteries." In China, we find the *chiang-shih*, a vampire with some strong resemblances to the types found in lands far distant from China. Such examples of vampires that are similar, yet in different geographic locations that could not possibly have traded beliefs, make a strong case for the existence of some truth to the vampire legend.

A *chiang-shih* was supposedly created when a person died in a violent way. It was believed that this soul could not rest, so it would return. The nocturnal creature that resulted was particularly vicious—the *chiang-shih* would tear its victims apart and feed upon them. The creature was also difficult to corner, as it could fly away into the night at any time.

Some of the biggest similarities the *chiang-shih* had with the vampires of the West were the methods used for thwarting its activities. Garlic and running water would keep it away, and fire was considered a good way to destroy the vampire. However, unlike the other vampires of the world, the *chiang-shih* could not leave its grave. It had to somehow escape before it was buried.

Surprisingly, the Chinese belief in vampires did not carry over to neighboring Japan. In fact, ancient Japanese folklore mentions only a slightly vampiric creature called the *kappa*, which lives in the water and pulls animals in to drink their blood. The legends and lore surrounding the creature do not contain any mention of the *kappa* as being an undead human.

Moving south in the Pacific, we come to the continent of Australia. The ancient aboriginals (who still live in the outback) believed in two types of vampire. The first was a creature that, like the *kappa*, was not undead. It was called the *yara-ma-yha-who*, and was described as a short creature that lived in fig trees. It would attack its victims by jumping down and draining their blood with its suction-cup-like fingers.

The other aboriginal belief in vampires is shown in their burial practices. When someone died, the others in the tribe would sit around the body, chanting throughout the entire night. They believed that the ritual and the fire they kept burning overnight would prevent evil spirits from entering the body and causing it to rise and harm the living.

Africa

Before we deal with the extensive vampire folklore of Europe, let's take a look at some important vampire beliefs further south. A particular species of vampire, called the *obayifo*, originated in Africa. Curiously enough, this creature has parallels in Newfoundland.

Unlike most vampires, the *obayifo* was not undead, but rather a living "witch" (no connection to Witches, the practitioners of Wicca who practice positive magic). The witch could leave her body at night and feed off the blood of sleeping victims. What's interesting about that is the possibility that the blood was just a metaphor for psychic energy, making the *obayifo* an intentional psychic vampire. The hag attack of Newfoundland that we will discuss later in the book was believed to be a similar type of attack.

Several other vampire-like witches are found in Africa. The similarities among them make it seem likely that one of two things occurred: Either the beliefs spread across the continent, or there really were people practicing psychic vampirism.

One non-human vampire creature is also found in Africa. That is the *asasabonsam*, a monster described as having ferocious iron teeth. Like the *yara-ma-yha-who*, the *asasabonsam* lived in trees and attacked from above.

As a final note to this section, many writers have used a center of mysticism in Africa—Egypt—as either the location of their vampire stories, or as the country of their vampires' origins. One popular example of the latter is Anne Rice's *Queen of the Damned*. However, in reality, there is no evidence to support the belief in an even remotely vampire-like creature in ancient Egypt.

Europe

No other area in the world is home to as great a collection of vampire lore as Europe. Among Europe's many countries, the legends of the undead (and possibly the undead themselves) have freely traveled, making it difficult to determine where the exact origin of the vampire legend in the continent was. For that reason, our starting point will be one of the oldest civilizations in Europe that was a center of learning and trade in the ancient world—Greece.

Ancient Greek myths and epics about many supernatural topics exist. Among them are a few tales of vampirism as well. Possibly the oldest story, and one that was directly linked to the gods of mythology, was that of Lamia. According to myth, Lamia was a mortal queen of Libya. She was apparently very beautiful, for the Greek god Zeus fell in love with Lamia when he saw her. He eventually fathered some of her children.

Zeus' wife, Hera, who is well known in mythology for her jealousy, soon found out about her husband's infidelity. Knowing that there was little she could do to the ruler of the Greek gods, Hera decided to take her revenge on Lamia by taking away all her children that Zeus sired. As can be expected, Lamia was enraged at this but, being a mortal, could not get even with Hera directly. So the queen decided that other mortal mothers should have to suffer as she did.

From that time on, Lamia wandered the world drinking the blood of young children. She was considered a demonic being for her actions, and soon after, the race of *lamiae* was named after her. Those vampires were described as female creatures with serpent-like bodies. It is unclear, however, if they were considered the later offspring of Lamia, or just vampires that acted as she did.

Some people in Greece still belive in vampires. This particular creature is known as the *vrykolakas*—a word originally used to denote a type of werewolf in Slavic countries.

A person could become a *vrykolakas* in the same way that other vampires discussed in the preceding sections are created. That is, through violent death or an improper burial. However, it was also a common belief in Greece (and in other Orthodox nations) that an excommunicated person (one who was banished from the Church and its sacraments) would not be able to find peace upon death. Apparently, whoever had that curse pronounced upon him or her by a priest would become a vampire as well. We'll look more closely at excommunication in the next chapter.

The *vrykolakas* seemed to have a predilection for attacking people it knew while alive. Often, the vampire would go to the houses of its friends and relatives and call their names from outside. To open the door was considered a more than fatal mistake, as the creature would attack whoever answered, causing him or her to become a vampire as well.

To destroy a *vrykolakas*, the traditional methods that have achieved an immortality of their own (in literature and on the big screen) were used. These methods are, of course, the driving of a wooden stake through the creature, and the removal of its head. The stake was used because it supposedly pinned the body of the creature to its grave so that it could not rise. As for the decapitation of the vampire, once it was accomplished, the head was often placed where it could not be reached by the *vrykolakas.* Those methods were sometimes followed by the burning of the body. Also, on occasion, if the undead was known to be excommunicated, this ban was lifted by a priest to grant peace to the *vrykolakas* (and to the village!).

I mentioned earlier that some people in Greece still believe in vampires. To back that statement, I have included in the next chapter a sworn account from an elderly Greek woman who is currently living in the United States. It is a tale of a *vrykolakas* who ravaged the village in which her mother lived. Apparently, people in the area still talk about it, almost a century later.

Greece's neighboring countries are also rich in vampire folklore. The citizens of Bulgaria, to the northeast, have beliefs that are similar to those of the Greeks. There too, vampires were created by violent deaths or by the inability of the soul of the deceased to find peace. In Bulgaria, however, excommunication was not the only thing that kept souls from reaching spiritual peace. The improper performance of a burial ritual could also be the cause.

Once the *vapir* or *ubour* (depending on the region) was formed, it would continue feasting on people in the area until disposed of by a *vampirdzhija*—a Bulgarian vampire hunter. Some were dealt with by use of a wooden stake, while some were apparently forced into bottles with an icon, or holy picture. The bottle was then tossed into a fire.

North of Bulgaria is the land most people associate with vampires immediately because it contains the district of Transylvania. The country is, of course, Romania. The general association of Transylvania with vampires is correct for the wrong reasons. While it is true that people in Transylvania do have well-developed beliefs in the undead, Transylvania was not the home of the real Dracula. Vlad Dracula (who is dealt with in Chapter Four) was the prince of another district of Romania, Wallachia.

In Romania, vampires are called *strigoi* or *strigoaica* (male and female, respectively). Like the vampires of Africa, some vampires in Romania are considered living witches who can leave their bodies to attack others. In fact, the Romanian word for witch is *striga*, which shows how the two are connected. Those living vampires are called *strigoi vii*, and like their African counterparts, might be psychic vampires.

Immortal blood-drinking vampires in the area are called *strigoi morti*. Those creatures are "traditional" vampires not only because they leave their graves at night and feed on the blood of the living, but also because of the ways they were destroyed. Romanians believed that *strigoi morti* could be thwarted by the methods that became popular in novels like *Dracula*. Garlic kept vampires away, the branch of the wild rose kept them from leaving their graves, and holy symbols would repel them. Of course, staking and decapitation were the preferred methods of destroying Romanian vampires.

Also from Romania comes the belief in the *nosferatu*, a creature whose etymology is more confusing than its nature. No matter where the name *nosferatu* came from, it is associated with a blood-drinking vampire that possesses the ability to have sexual relations with the living. A person is doomed to become a *nosferatu* if he or she is the illegitimate child of illegitimately born parents. The usual vampire-killing methods used in Europe are also used to destroy the *nosferatu*.

For space considerations, some vampires resembling the ones we just examined, and which are found in eastern European nations that neighbor Romania, will be left out of our examination. However, we will take a look at two northeastern countries in the continent whose inhabitants believe in a different type of vampire.

In Poland and Russia, we find folklore that deals with the *upior* or *upyr* (Polish and Russian, respectively). Both creatures have a trait that makes them unique among the vampires of the world—they attack and roam from noon to midnight, which means at least half their activity occurs during daylight hours! Although sunlight is not destructive to vampires according to folklore (that was made popular by fiction writers), it is still uncommon for an undead to hunt for its victims during waking hours.

Despite their unusual hours of activity, the *upior* and *upyr* were still similar to other traditional vampires in that they had a ceaseless bloodthirst. Both creatures were disposed of in the traditional European ways, although Russians would also pour holy water on the *upyr* when they found it in its coffin.

Some countries with vampires resembling those found in Romania, Bulgaria, and even Greece lie to the west. In Germany, the *nachtzehrer* behaves in an almost identical fashion to the *vrykolakas*. However, the former were known to feed on the bodies of the dead as well as on the blood of the living.

From the Hungarian province of Serbia comes the famous vampire case of Peter Plogojowitz, which is discussed in the next chapter. Because that account accurately illustrates the Hungarian belief in vampires, no more on that region will be included here.

Great Britain and France do not have any notable, original vampire folklore, although England has had a couple of famous vampire cases over the past two hundred years (relevant ones will be examined later in this book).

Let me reiterate that several European countries not mentioned in this section do have some type of vampire folklore, but were not included because of their similarity. Italy, for example, has an ancient belief in a living vampire, the *strega*, which behaves in a similar manner to the *strigoi vii* of Romania. The purpose of this chapter is not to provide a comprehensive look at every bit of vampire lore in the world, but to describe the folkloric beliefs which have direct relevance to our uncovering the truth behind the legends, in later chapters.

North and South America

The New World is not without its own vampire lore. Several cultures in the southern part of the western hemisphere believed in the undead, and the similarity of those beliefs with the ones of other countries across the oceans makes a good argument for their possible truth.

In South America, we find another living vampire that could possibly be a psychic vampire—the *asema*. Again, this was a sorcerer who could leave his or her body in some form at night and feed upon others.

Moving north, we come to Mexico, a land that contains some notable vampire lore because of the cultures that once inhabited the region. The Aztecs had a belief in female vampire beings called the *cihuateteo*. Like many other female vampiric entities, a *cihuateteo* was created when a woman died in childbirth. The vampires would roam and attack children, as did the *lamiae* of Greece.

Also in Mexico, is yet another living vampire, the *tlahuelpuchi*, which also makes a strong case for the existence of psychic vampires. This was a person who could somehow transform him or herself and feed off others. Once again, the transformation could be a metaphor for astral projection.

Finally, when examining the United States and Canada, it quickly becomes evident that there is no ancient, native vampire folklore in the area. The Native American Indians, who were the earliest verifiable inhabitants of the continent, have little or no mention of vampires or the undead in their folklore. It is safe to assume that the first vampire beliefs (and maybe vampires!) probably came to North America with the settlers.

While a few cases of vampirism in America have been documented within the past two hundred years, we will not be dealing with any of them in this chapter. Some of the case histories described later, along with the letters from mortal blood drinkers, will explain the vampire beliefs and recent legends of North America.

Before we conclude our worldwide look, let me make a few things clear about vampirism in the United States and Canada. From the information I have gathered (and which I will share in the pages that follow), I have found that psychic vampirism seems to be the predominant type of vampire attack found in North America. Briefly, here are a couple of examples of beliefs that have developed folkloric status.

In the southern states of America, there is a belief in a spirit called a "haint." People are sometimes warned by their friends and relatives (often in a joking way) not to sleep on their backs or a haint will "get them." Being attacked by a haint is similar to the attack pattern of other psychic vampires (remember, an example of one of those types of attack is given in the Introduction).

One other example of possible psychic vampirism is found in Newfoundland, Canada. The order of beings that are responsible for vampirism is called (by at least some of the people who live there) "Old Hags." For that reason, the attack for which they are responsible has been dubbed the "Hag Attack."

Like the *strigoi vii*, the vampires of Newfoundland are believed to be witches or sorcerers who can leave their bodies and attack others. What's interesting about the documented cases of Hag Attack, however, is that blood drinking is never mentioned, even as a metaphor for psychic vampirism. The belief in this form of psychic vampire became so common over the years that some who live in Newfoundland developed ways of preventing the attack.

Just how common is psychic vampirism in Newfoundland? David J. Hufford, the folklorist, reported in his excellent book *The Terror that Comes in the Night*, the results of a survey he conducted among residents of Newfoundland. He distributed a questionnaire that described the most basic form of that experience in the question: "Have you ever awakened during the night to find yourself paralyzed, i.e., unable to move or cry out?" Later questions further defined the experience (which is examined in Chapter Seven), but for now, it should suffice to say that 23 percent of the people to whom he gave his questionnaire had experienced at least that basic form of Hag Attack, one or more times in their lives.

Chapter Three

Immortal Blood Drinkers

We've all seen the typical vampire hunter of fiction. He or she is armed with a crucifix, a wooden stake, and perhaps a vial of holy water or a bit of sacred wafer. Often, the hands that hold those items are trembling, and the look on the face of their holder is anything but one of confidence. Yet the hunter still enters the graveyard or castle lair of the vampire (often, too close to sunset for comfort), and eventually finds the undead. A struggle might then ensue, although sometimes the mortal is lucky enough to dispose of the fiend before it can awaken.

Interestingly, the vampire hunters portrayed in books and movies are not much different from their historical counterparts. It is the "real-life" vampires and their surroundings that are different. Forget about the castles shown in the movies. Also forget about the eerie night-time encounters with the undead, or any struggles they might give upon being discovered. The real-life hunters had it much easier.

The only lair the hunters visited was a graveyard (in the daytime, and in large numbers); the only foes they faced were bodies that did not come to life in any way, yet displayed "obvious signs of the vampire condition." Strange things were reported when bodies were staked, but an alleged vampire never attacked a hunter. Were those corpses really undead, or simply mistaken as such by people who couldn't possibly know any better given their medical knowledge?

In this chapter we'll attempt to answer that question by examining documented cases of immortal blood drinkers in folklore. Because most of the witnesses discussed in the cases in this chapter were the hunters themselves, it seemed only fitting to begin this discussion with their mention. Of course, there are also the testimonies of the victims who managed to survive a vampire's attack for at least one night. However, these accounts were often taken down by the hunters, who might have been influenced by their own preconceived notions.

The following should become evident shortly: Of the four types of vampires described in this book, the evidence that supports the existence of immortal blood drinkers is the weakest, primarily because of its age (the most recent case in this chapter is seventy-five years old). "Facts" reported many years ago are not verifiable and cannot always be accepted blindly (neither can "facts" reported today, for that matter; tabloids are proof of that).

Therefore, please explore the following pages with an open mind. Both sides of the evidence will be presented in each case: the eye-witness accounts, as well as some possible non-vampiric explanations for the phenomena. Finally, when our examination of the cases is complete, we'll take a look at some of the occult theories put forth that attempt to explain the existence of immortal blood drinkers.

You might notice that a few of the vampires mentioned in this chapter display some phantom-like attributes. In fact, one of them, Peter Plogojowitz, was mentioned in Chapter One as just such a vampire. However, phantom-like attributes do not necessarily make a creature a psychic vampire. Because blood drinking was associated with the aforementioned case, and because the alleged undead was disposed of in the same way as other immortal blood drinkers, the case is included here.

The case that follows is familiar and interesting for a number of reasons, but let's allow the facts to speak for themselves.

Arnold Paole and His Successors

This is one of the instances in folklore where a person is turned into a vampire by another such creature. Arnold Paole was a Serbian soldier who lived in the early 1700s. While alive, he admitted that he witnessed and was part of some ghastly occurrences. Paole said that while he was in Gossowa (in Turkish Serbia), he was attacked by a vampire. The people of that area and era believed that the only way to rid oneself of a troublesome vampire was to eat some of the earth from its grave and smear oneself with the creature's blood. Paole claimed to have done just that, although it is unclear how he obtained some of the vampire's blood.

Apparently, the method worked as a deterrent but not as a cure. Paole was able to return to his home in 1727; however, he died soon after from a fall off a haywagon, and was buried. Within a month after Paole's death, the people of his village started reporting that he was attacking them at night. Four of the victims eventually died.

The villagers began to fear the vampire, and decided to dig up his body. When the "hunters" did so, they found that Paole's body was undecayed, his skin and nails had fallen away and had been replaced by new skin and nails, and (of course) streams of "fresh blood" were flowing from his orifices. To rid themselves of the monster, the villagers drove a wooden stake through Paole, and according to them, the vampire groaned and blood erupted from his body. They then burned the body.

Paole never again bothered anyone, but the hunters were still not satisfied that the curse was lifted from their village. They believed that all of Paole's victims were also vampires, and to make sure the village was free from vampires for good, the hunters dug up those bodies as well. They found them also to be in the "vampire condition," and disposed of them in the same manner.

Several years later, another epidemic apparently broke out, because another vampire hunt occurred in the same graveyard. In the account of that expedition, *Visum et Repertum*, which is translated in Paul Barber's book *Vampires, Burial, and Death*, sixteen alleged vampires were exhumed. All of the "successors" of Paole seemed to have the same characteristics as he did (lack of decomposition, new skin and nails, and the presence of fresh blood). Also, all the vampires were buried for approximately the same amount of time—around two months.

Four of the vampires were infants, and three of them were buried along with their mothers (who were among the alleged sixteen vampires). The belief that a vampire's child would also become a vampire was common in Greece as well (see "The *Vrykolakas* of Pyrgos" later in this chapter).

There is no surviving written testimony of just what Paole's victims saw, or of how they were attacked by him. The only evidence we have is the secondary source already mentioned, the *Visum et Repertum*. That is a secondary account because it was written by the hunters who investigated Paole's successors. How reliable is this source for determining what actually happened at the graveyard in either instance?

There is no accurate way to determine that for certain, but something is clear: Even if the hunters in both instances did see exactly what they reported, that still does not provide actual evidence for the existence of immortal blood drinkers. Here's why.

The vampire hunters of years ago did not possess the medical knowledge we have today. When they exhumed bodies in those days and commented on their appearance, the hunters did not exactly have anything to compare that physical condition to. The only partially decomposed corpses they might have come across, besides those of "vampires," were ones that were accidentally discovered in remote locations, and which animals or the elements had helped along in decomposition. Even medical doctors in Europe at the time did not have a good knowledge of how decomposition progressed in a human corpse.

Add to that lack of knowledge the superstitious beliefs of the investigators, and it becomes easy to doubt their judgment. In many countries, it was believed that the soul of a person remained among the living for forty days. For that period of time, many cultures practiced strict mourning and various traditions, such as covering all the mirrors in a house until the spirit was gone. However, after the forty-day period ended, the general belief was that the soul would move on, and the corpse would consequently decompose.

Various occult theories either agree or disagree with the theory that souls remain among the living for forty days; however, no modern scientific theory supports the idea that a corpse should fully decompose after forty days. Decomposition actually begins a few hours after death, as free-radicals begin to have free reign over the organism, and decay is accelerated by bacteria and other parasites. Decomposition to skeletal remains can take several months or even years, depending on a large number of factors. Also, the process does not resemble what the vampire hunters of yesterday expected.

Therefore, even though Arnold Paole was discovered in a "non-decomposed" state, according to the account we have, it is the perception of decomposition or the lack thereof that is important. The fact that Paole's body was not a skeleton after forty days would probably have been enough to make the hunters believe they were seeing a vampire. However, that was not all they found. Paole's skin and nails had fallen away and were replaced with new skin and nails. Despite what the hunters thought, that evidence is also not conclusive.

When a corpse decomposes, the state of its tissues changes. Sometimes, outer layers of skin fall off as the inner layers begin to liquefy. The inner layers would often have a ruddy appearance, and could appear to be "new skin" to someone who didn't know better. Also, nails, and eventually hair, begin to fall off a decomposing body. The shape of the skin under the nails could look as if new nails were forming.

As for the last vampiric characteristic of Paole's body— the flowing of blood from the orifices—there is also a scientific explanation. During decomposition, gases build up in a corpse, causing many strange-looking things to occur (some of which are mentioned in later cases). As the gases continue to build, the body begins to swell. At the same time, liquefaction of the internal tissues and organs continues. The pressure from the gases could cause the resulting dark liquids (not really pure blood) to be forced from the body through the areas of least resistance (the eyes, the nostrils, and of course, the mouth).

While we're discussing the swelling of the body, a couple of things should be mentioned. If the swelling is observed in its early stages (before the body begins to look unusually distended) or in its late stages (after it has begun to subside),the body would have the appearance of being quite whole. In fact, a deceased elderly person might even look younger because any wrinkles or discolorations would seem to have vanished. Because Paole's hunters (and those who came after) expected to find little more than bones, a slightly bloated corpse could look like it was alive.

Also, the bloating would cause one other characteristic noticed in this case. When the body of Arnold Paole was staked, it emitted a groan and a large amount of blood. Both of these occurrences could have been caused by the sudden expelling of gas and liquid that had built up in the body. Driving a stake into a body in that state of decomposition would be like popping a water balloon with a pin.

That about covers both sides of the Paole case. As you can see, because we can't be sure of exactly what Paole's alleged victims experienced, we are left with nothing more than observations of a corpse that could have been decomposing naturally. So the question of whether or not Arnold Paole was a vampire remains unanswered. It is interesting to remember that once his body was destroyed, there were no more instances of vampirism attributed to him. Of course, if superstitious fear is the only thing that made the villagers think Paole was a vampire in the first place, simply reporting that his body was destroyed would probably have had the same peace-giving effect.

To continue our examination of immortal blood drinkers, we'll look at one of Paole's fellow countrymen who also entered the pages of history as a possible vampire; his story follows.

Peter Plogojowitz

This case of vampirism took place in a section of Serbia that later became part of Hungary. If you recall from the last chapter, I mentioned that this case accurately illustrates the beliefs of the people from that area. That is because the hunters in this account conveyed their feelings to an impartial observer, who then prepared a record of the incident in a thorough manner. The amount of evidence present in the case makes a strong argument for the existence of immortal blood drinkers if viewed alone. However, as in the other cases in this chapter, the possible non-occult explanations weaken the case. Some of the characteristics of this incident are similar to those of the previous one.

The incident took place in the village of Kisilova around the mid-1720s. It should be noted, before proceeding, that the facts are taken from the eyewitness report of the Imperial Provisor of the region. He was present, along with the Gradisk parish priest (called a pope), at the exhumation of the "vampire." Whether that makes the information any more reliable than accounts of other incidents remains to be seen. Unfortunately, the victims' accounts of what happened were not recorded in a manner that lends them credibility (there are no surviving quotes from any of those attacked, although one of the victims was identified).

Peter Plogojowitz, the alleged vampire, died (it's not clear of what) and was buried. He was in his grave for about ten weeks when the villagers reported seeing him at night. They claimed that he came to them while they were in their beds and attacked them (it is Plogojowitz's alleged materializations in the houses of others that made him a phantom-like vampire). Some victims indicated that the vampire suffocated them. Overall, nine people died within a week.

The general panic worsened when Plogojowitz's wife claimed to have seen her husband. She said that he came to her asking for his shoes (it was a common belief in Europe that vampires desired certain earthly possessions). The woman was so terrified by the encounter that she left the village. After that, the people decided to exhume Plogojowitz's body to dispose of him as a threat once and for all.

The Imperial Provisor who reported the incident was at first against the idea of the vampire hunt, but he saw that the people could not be discouraged. So he and the parish priest went to the graveyard. When the body was exhumed, the first thing they noticed was that it was odor-free. They also noticed that the body was not decomposed and was whole, except for the nose, which had fallen away. Also, Plogojowitz's skin had fallen away, and new skin was growing. The same was true for his nails. Finally, there was blood flowing from his mouth.

To destroy the body, the traditional stake was used. When it was driven through the "vampire," plenty of what was believed to be fresh blood issued forth from the body. The body also displayed some "wild signs" which were not made clear in the report. After the staking, the body was burned and the village was no longer troubled.

To avoid repetition, it should be noted that several of the preceding observations can be explained with the arguments presented in the last case. As for the lack of odor, that could depend on a number of factors. It is not clear during what time of year the incident took place. However, if it were winter, it is hard to imagine someone detecting the scent of an exhumed body amid a crowd of people who lived in a less-sanitary time, and who were probably carrying torches. Finally, the condition of the corpse's nose should be noted. Because the nose is shaped by cartilage alone, it is easy to imagine what would happen to that shape after a body had bloated.

As you might have noticed, the similarities between the last two cases resulted in a need for fewer necessary "rational" explanations in the latter one. However, some cases in this chapter seem to defy rational explanation. The next one is a good example. It also takes place in Hungary (we will, of course, deal with cases from other areas of Europe, but for now, keeping tales from related areas together serves as a means of comparison).

The Vampires of Haidamaque

Augustine Calmet, in his hard-to-find *The Phantom World*, describes a case that, if true, provides some strong evidence for the existence of immortal blood drinkers. Part of the reason for that is the number of years the alleged vampires in the story had already been dead (or perhaps, undead). The following events were reported in 1730 by the Count de Cabreras, who was the captain of the Alandetti infantry of Hungary. However, they were supposed to have occurred around the year 1715 (the early 1700s was apparently a popular time for vampirism in Europe). This is one of the few cases of vampirism where a count mentioned in the story is not the vampire.

Some of the count's men were temporarily stationed in the town of Haidamaque, and were consequently staying with the villagers (a common practice at that time). One of the soldiers (whose name is not mentioned) was sitting at a table one day with his host (the master of the house) and some of the man's friends and/or family (it is not clear exactly who the others were). On that evening, a man the soldier did not recognize came in and sat down at the table next to the master of the house. Everyone at the table seemed very nervous at his coming, and the soldier wasn't sure why that was so.

The next morning, the soldier woke up and found that his host was dead. Curious, the soldier asked if the strange visitor had anything to do with it. The others in the house told the soldier that the man who appeared was the host's father, who had been dead and buried for ten years! Apparently, they believed he had come to take his son.

Upon hearing that, the soldier informed the others in his regiment, who then contacted the Count de Cabreras. The count was intrigued enough by the report to go to the house with some of his men and a surgeon to check the facts for himself. Satisfied that the inhabitants of the house, along with the rest of the village, believed the story to be true, he went with his expedition to the graveyard. They located the grave of the house master's father, and removed the body.

The alleged vampire discovered in the grave seemed to be completely undecayed, as if he were still alive. There was no mention of skin and nails having fallen off and growing back. Also, it is mentioned in the report that his blood was like that of a living man. That was probably an afterthought caused by what happened next. The count had his soldiers cut off the vampire's head, and the preceding statement probably indicates that there was a heavy flow of blood as a result.

After the vampire was disposed of, the count asked if there were any other such creatures in the vicinity. The villagers told him of a couple of instances of vampirism. The first was a man who had died more than thirty years before. He had come back to his own house on three occasions (all of them mealtime). The first time, the vampire attacked and drank the blood of his brother, who died instantly. The next two times, he did the same to his son and a servant, respectively. Both died as well. When they exhumed the body of that vampire, they found it to be in the same condition as the first. This time, however, the count had his men drive a nail into the head of the creature.

The other vampire the villagers mentioned was a man who had died about sixteen years before. That vampire supposedly drank the blood of his two sons, killing both of them. When they removed that body from the grave, they found that it was in a similar vampiric condition. The count, who apparently liked to vary his methods of vampire killing, ordered that the creature be burned.

If the eyewitnesses in the preceding case are telling the truth, and if the dates have not been distorted, there is no way the events described could be attributed to the lack of medical knowledge on the part of the count and his hunters. A body that has been in the ground for ten years could not in any way resemble that of a living person. The state of decay in the corpses buried for sixteen and thirty years would be, logically, even worse. Unfortunately, the case happened too long ago to be verified, but if taken at face value, the preceding account does seem to prove the existence of immortal blood drinkers, doesn't it?

As promised, let's now look at a couple of cases from other regions in Europe, starting with this tale from England. If you recall, I mentioned that England has no original folklore concerning the undead. However, as this incident shows, immortal blood drinkers could have walked on English soil at one time.

The Croglin Grange Vampire

Like all the cases in this chapter, this is a tale that can't be proven. With re-telling, stories often become a little more exciting than they might have been. Eventually, the original facts can be lost even by the storytellers, making some stories in folklore a little hard to accept as truth.

The case of the Croglin Grange Vampire is a good candidate for a story that might have been altered with re-telling. An account of it appeared in Augustine Hare's book *Story of My Life* in the late 1890s. Although it was not told to him by an actual witness, Hare felt that it must be true and wrote it down. How much of the story has a basis in fact is anyone's guess.

According to Hare's account, Croglin Grange was a house in Cumberland (modern-day Cumbria), England. While no record or remains of such a place exist, the house seems to be a reference to the real Low Croglin Hall of the area.

Sometime in the mid-1870s, the owners of Croglin Grange, the Fisher family, rented the large one-story house to three (un-named) tenants—two brothers and their sister—among a few others. On one night in the first summer the three spent in the house, the young woman decided not to close the shutters on her window. As she lay in bed, she had a clear view from her house to the belt of trees that separated the church-yard from her yard. She noticed there were two bizarre lights moving in a weaving manner between the trees. In a few moments, the lights emerged from the tree belt, and she real-ized they were the eyes of some dark, humanoid creature.

The young woman sat up in bed, terrified, as she noticed the thing running across the lawn toward the house. Every so often it would vanish into the shadows, only to re-emerge, closer than before. She wanted to scream, but her voice was paralyzed with terror; she wanted to run to her bedroom door, but the window was too close to it and she feared that the thing might be able to see her.

Eventually, the creature seemed to change course, and the woman thought it was running around the house. She immedi-ately jumped out of bed and ran to her bedroom door, appar-ently hoping to get to her brothers, but when she reached the door, she heard a strange scratching at her window, and turned to it. The thing was right outside her window. It had what she would later describe as a hideous brown face with flaming eyes, and it was staring right at her. She screamed and ran back to her bed.

She noticed the creature had started picking at one of the panes in the window, and in moments, one of the pieces of glass fell into the room. The vampire then put its hand in through the window, unlocked it, and opened it. Within seconds, it was in the room and standing over her. It immediately grabbed her by the hair, pulled her head back, and bit into her throat. She screamed loudly, and in a few seconds, her brothers came running to her locked bedroom door and broke it down.

When they entered the room, the two men found their sister lying in bed, unconscious and with her neck bleeding. The vampire was in the process of escaping through the open window. One brother chased it into the woods and noticed that it seemed to disappear over the wall of the churchyard. The other brother tended to his injured sister.

Later, when the woman recovered consciousness, she commented that her attacker was probably some lunatic who had escaped from an asylum. The doctor who examined her the next day felt that she had suffered a great shock, and, regardless of what had caused it, some change in her surroundings would do her much good. So the three decided to go away to Switzerland. They stayed there until the autumn, when the young woman decided that she would like to return, commenting that lunatics do not escape from asylums every day.

She stayed in the same room upon her return, but started closing her shutters from then on. However, the shutters were of the type that did not cover the top pane of the window. One night in March, she heard a scratching again. When she looked out the top pane, she saw the same brown face with the flaming eyes looking at her. She screamed immediately this time, and her brothers, who were ready for such an occasion, ran out the front of the house with pistols. They chased the creature, and one of the brothers managed to shoot it in the leg. The vampire still made it over the churchyard fence, however, and the two watched it vanish into an old, decrepit vault.

The next morning, the brothers went with all the other tenants in the house to the churchyard. There they opened the suspected vault and found that all of the coffins within had been opened and their contents ripped out. One coffin alone was untouched. The group immediately went to that coffin and opened it.

Inside they found the vampire. They described it as being shriveled, brown, and mummified in appearance. On its leg was the mark of a pistol shot, which positively identified the creature to the brothers who had chased and shot it. To destroy the vampire, the group took it out and burned it.

The authenticity of the above story is questionable, as is the case with many folktales of vampirism. However, like those other tales, there might be some truth in it. What makes the story most interesting is the description given of the vampire. Descriptions of brown, mummified-looking vampires with shriveled skin are not exactly common in folklore. There is the possibility, however, that the "vampire" was little more than just a decaying corpse, which would explain the creature's appearance, but not the story of the two young men and their sister. What motive they would have for making up such a story is anyone's guess. We will never know for certain if this story is true or false.

Let's say that the three were telling the truth, and really did witness the strange occurrences already described. The case of the Croglin Grange Vampire would then be the first documented instance of vampirism where the attacking vampire was physically proven to be the same entity as the corpse exhumed by a hunting party. The bullet wound found in the creature's leg might very well be the first piece of evidence to put a vampire at the "scene of the crime."

There is still controversy over whether the Croglin Grange Vampire was factual or fictional. The people in the area, as well as researchers from around the world, have differing opinions about the famous case. However, not every case of vampirism is disbelieved after its occurrence. I have learned of a particular incident that as recently as the mid-1970s was definitely accepted as having occurred, although I haven't been able to ascertain if that is still so in the mid-1990s.

What follows is the story of an undead who terrorized a village in Greece in the early 1920s. Unlike the cases that preceded it, this one was told to me by an eyewitness' daughter, who heard of the incident from her mother and many others in the area throughout her life in the country. As you shall see, the case wonderfully illustrates the general beliefs that Greek people have about vampires.

The Vrykolakas of Pyrgos

The following story was told to me by a Greek woman who I shall call E. I learned about this incident from a family member who knows her, and asked E. about it. My talk with her, which took place in Greek (in which I am fluent), was somewhat long. E. gave a lot of unimportant details, and it would have been impossible to give a verbatim, translated account of our talk here. For that reason, I have extracted only the facts from her tale, and have organized them into a third-person telling of the story. Words within quotation marks are an exact translation of a statement made by E.

E.'s mother, who we shall call M., was approximately twenty-one years old when the following incident occurred (circa 1922). She was living with her husband and their two-year-old son (E. wasn't born for another three years), in the village of Pyrgos, which is located on the western shore of the Peloponnesus in Greece. That village has since flourished and has a modern-day population of over 21,000, although in the 1920s it was just a small farming village. Like many other small farming villages, Pyrgos was a place where everyone knew everyone else.

One particular farmer (name unknown) in the village of Pyrgos was apparently suffering from some kind of serious depression in the year 1922; he began drinking a lot toward the end of the last harvest. His wife began to worry about him, and told several people in the village about her husband's misery, probably in hopes that someone would help him. It is unclear whether anyone approached the young man at the outset of his problem; however, if someone did, it didn't work. He would come home later and later each night, drunk, and would become violent if his wife asked him about it.

The woman's misery then started to show on her face. M. told E. that she was able to "see the woman's sadness clearer each passing day." Word started getting around the small village (as gossip often does in such places) of the young man's late nights out. When one of the young man's friends finally decided to talk to him about it one afternoon in the field, the farmer made light of the whole situation, saying that he liked drinking beneath the old olive tree at the end of the field at night.

One evening, the farmer's wife invited another couple over for dinner (the husband was the same friend who talked to the young farmer earlier). That night, M. and her husband went to the house to check on the distraught wife. Seeing that the woman had company, M. told her that she and her husband would leave as soon as the farmer got home from the fields for dinner. As it grew later, and the food became colder, "the four tried to make the sad woman cheerful, as best as they could." At around ten o'clock, M. and her husband left; the husband had still not come home.

What happened after would soon be known by everyone in the village. By eleven o'clock, the wife was extremely upset, saying that her husband had never come home that late before. The male dinner guest, who apparently couldn't stand to see the woman cry anymore, said that he would find the man and bring him home. Remembering what the man had told him a few days before, he immediately headed for the olive tree that was supposedly his friend's drinking spot.

When the man got to the spot, he found an empty bottle of wine, which he recognized as a common type sold by one of the town's merchants. However, there wasn't much time for the man to think about the bottle and the fact that his friend had probably been drinking again, because a creaking sound alerted him, and he turned around. "Hanging by the neck from a rope tied to the branch of a tall tree" was a dark figure the man immediately recognized as his friend.

The wife's grief at learning of her husband's death was made worse when she spoke to the priest of the village about it the next day. He told her what she already knew, but refused to accept: As one who has committed suicide, her husband was to be "buried in unconsecrated ground, without the burial prayers," and was to be considered excommunicated from the Greek Orthodox Church. In that time, the Church was a major part of the people's lives, and to be removed from it, even after death, was not taken lightly. The woman, along with several other villagers (M. included), believed that the young man's soul would never find rest, and that his body would never "melt" or decompose. She begged the priest to spare her husband that fate, but he would not hear her pleas. The man was ritualistically "removed from the Church" (excommunicated) and buried just outside the cemetery.

For the next two months, the woman was in mourning and kept to herself most of the time. After those two months, however, M. and the others in the village noticed that the woman completely stopped speaking with anyone, and almost never left her house. The villagers attributed her strange behavior to the "insanity that comes over those in mourning." But the people in the village could not be concerned with the woman's behavior for long, as they had other things to worry about.

After the same two-month period, a strange plague appeared in the town. Within a week, eight people were forced to remain in bed due to "loss of strength," and two died. Nervous villagers commented on how the ill claimed to have been "shaken" and bitten by something in their beds at night. No connection was made by the villagers to the recent suicide of the young farmer.

After that first plague week, the same woman who had stayed with the widow on the night of her husband's suicide went to see if she needed anything. When the woman told the widow the news of the plague, she broke down and replied, terrified, that her husband had returned to her late every night and had "lain with her" until the early morning hours for the entire past week. The shocked woman begged the widow to go to the priest and tell him. After a while, the widow, "who did not like the priest since her trauma," finally agreed to do just that.

No one knows exactly what the priest said to the woman when he heard of her "sins;" however, many witnessed what happened after. The priest immediately gathered some men from the village to go with him to the grave of the *vrykolakas* outside of the cemetery "to do God's work;" the women were not allowed to go near the site.

The method the men planned on using to destroy the vampire was particularly gruesome; they wanted to cut off his limbs, remove his heart, and burn his entire mutilated corpse. "With the help of God, they wanted to destroy the *vrykolakas* quickly." However, when the men got to the gravesite and exhumed the body, how quickly they acted is unclear. They would soon find quite a surprise.

The young man had been buried for two months, and appeared "shriveled and hardened," as if he were a skeleton with only a thin layer of "wrinkled flesh." However, there was something about the thing that made the men very uneasy. "Even the priest could not touch the thing for a great [length of] time." Finally, the priest started to say a prayer and began to advance on the body with his crucifix and Bible. The others followed.

At first, the dismembering of the corpse proceeded as planned. But when they opened the creature's chest, the men became frightened. Inside it, they found "melted" remains, and a completely preserved heart "that was beating still [!]" At that point, the priest took out a small bottle of holy water and poured it over the heart. As he did so, "the heart began to melt" and the *vrykolakas'* torso trembled until the heart was completely liquefied. By that time, some of the other men had already lit a large fire, so the group picked up the pieces of the creature and tossed them into the blaze, where they "caught fire like pieces of dry wood."

Even though the two who had died that week from the vampire's plague were buried according to the laws of the Church, the villagers and the priest decided to take the precaution of burning the bodies. They did so, and reread the burial prayers over the re-interred ashes. When the group returned to the village, they learned that those who were sick in bed were already "feeling much better and moving around again."

Things were quiet in the village for the next two months, and even the widow seemed to be acting like herself, although she was still sad. Then, one day, the widow's friend came to her house so they could walk to the village together. The widow apparently "knew that she was pregnant with the *vrykolakas'* baby [!]"

Soon the whole town knew, although it is unclear who spread the word. The priest watched over the widow very carefully for her entire term. When she finally gave birth, almost a year after her husband's death, it was clear to him exactly what had happened. He and the widow's friend finally learned the meaning of what the widow meant by her statement that her husband had "lain with her" every night for the week of his return.

The baby looked like the "monster that was his father." It died only seconds after being born, and the priest took it away from its mother to take certain precautions before burying it. After that, the town was once again at peace, and the widow, probably under the advice of the priest, entered an Orthodox convent "to pray for her sins" for the rest of her earthly days.

According to E., the preceding account varied slightly in details each time she heard it (as all folktales do). Some of the elements of the story do seem a bit dramatic, but there is no way to know for certain which elements, if any, were made up over the years. One thing is certain: the basic elements of the story were considered factual by those in the area of Pyrgos as recently as the mid-1970s, when E. left Greece to be with her family in America. It is quite possible that people living there today still talk of it, although I haven't been able to verify whether that is so. If what E. remembered of the story is accurate, and her parents and others were telling the truth, then it seems the villagers of Pyrgos witnessed some amazing things.

Can the events just discussed be explained in a non-occult way? Is there what some would consider a "rational explanation" for the *vrykolakas* of Pyrgos? There are other possible non-occult causes for each of the events above, although when put together they don't seem to account for the whole folktale. Let's look at them individually.

For starters, there is no reason to disbelieve the excommunication and unsanctified burial of the man who committed suicide. That was simply what was done in such a case. As for the plague that came two months later, it's quite possible that the people of Pyrgos really did come down with some disease. Maybe the disease caused hallucinations in those afflicted, causing them to feel as if they were under attack or being bitten (E. wasn't sure if there were bite marks on the victims or not). Perhaps the widow herself came down with a strain of the disease and only imagined that her husband came to her at night.

As for the condition of the body found in the grave, the shriveled appearance, depending on the climate, could be the result of a natural decomposition. Of course, the beating heart could not be explained if the people present really saw it. I suppose it is also possible that the villagers all became well that same day, although it seems a bit unlikely. Again, maybe the belief that the "monster" was destroyed could have made them well again.

What about the baby who was born too long after his father's death? There is the slight chance that the baby was simply two months overdue, although that is a rare possibility. Also, the grieving widow could have either willingly sought out "comforting" from, or have been taken advantage of by, another man in her time of sorrow. Perhaps she feared that her sin would be found out by those in Pyrgos, and made up the story of her husband coming back to her just in case she was pregnant. Either way, we can never know for certain.

But what if the story is true? What if an immortal blood drinker did terrorize those in Greece as recently as 1922? If that or any of the other incidents in this chapter really occurred, then modern biological science wouldn't have the answer as to what caused those vampires to come into being. For answers like that, we'd have to look to another science.

Some Occult Explanations

The existence of psychic vampires has been theorized upon to a great extent by many occultists, myself included. That is a result of the abundance of information, both old and new, that is available to the researcher. Like a physical scientist, an occultist also records observations and comes to a hypothesis, which he or she then tests and considers a theory. That could not be done to a great degree with the cases of immortal blood drinkers.

The vampires dealt with in this chapter do not seem to be active today, as we have already discussed. For that reason, the theories we have regarding their existence are somewhat dated, and relatively few in number. Let's look at those theories, old and new, in light of modern occult knowledge.

First of all, there were the sensationalistic views that vampires were created by the Devil to torment the living. That was apparently just a belief and not rationally thought out. Later, a theory would come from that belief, and it is worth mentioning here; it is one that some religions would also adopt.

Almost everyone has heard of demonic possession, thanks in part to *The Exorcist*. However, few have thought of the possibility that a demon, or evil entity, could take possession of a human body after death. If that were the case, it might need some physical substance to maintain the corpse in a magical way as its host. That substance would naturally be blood (we'll look at the occult power of blood in a moment).

Demonic possession after death as an explanation of vampirism accounts for why holy symbols repel vampires in folklore. Also, it makes it easier to understand why the body of a loved one would find it so easy to kill its family members when it became a vampire. The moral dilemmas faced by Anne Rice's vampires would be non-existent because the mind of the once-living individual would not be controlling the revenant corpse. Instead, it would be the mind of a demon who never cared for any of its victims in the first place.

That first theory should seem possible to anyone who accepts the existence of entities (for a detailed explanation of the nature of entities, see my first book, *Summoning Spirits: The Art of Magical Evocation*, also published by Llewellyn). However, the theory does not account for why a demon would do such a thing; one has to draw his or her own conclusions about that. If demons really do animate corpses, we can assume they do it for the same reason they would possess a living body—to terrorize the living. The weakness of the theory is that it is difficult to prove demonic possession exists at all, let alone in a corpse.

Before we look at more possible causes of vampirism, let's first examine some basic occult principles that might be applied to any explanation of the phenomenon. To start, there is the mystical power of blood. Countless rituals, both ancient and modern, use blood in some way, usually to accomplish one of two things: to represent the infusion or generation of magical power, or to represent the presence of the individual from whom the blood was taken.

The first use of blood in magic reflects the ancient belief that eventually found its way into the Bible and fiction as the statement "For the blood is the life." That belief came from the observation even the earliest people made—when someone lost all of his or her blood, he or she died. The earliest magicians believed that the loss of blood mystically caused death because of loss of energy, and did not attribute it to the lack of circulation. Of course, they were wrong in assuming that, but they might not have been wrong in considering blood to be a mystical, power-infused liquid.

Blood keeps us alive. Our lifeforce is maintained by its internal flow. Conversely, when someone bleeds to death, his or her lifeforce weakens in proportion to the flow of blood out of the body. There is what is known in the occult field as a "sympathetic link" between blood and life. Sympathetic links are established when something can be used to represent something else. In this case, blood naturally represents lifeforce, because the presence of the latter depends on the former.

Most people have heard of "voodoo dolls." This sort of doll is usually made with the hair, nails, clothing, or even blood of a person, and represents that individual to the point where anything done to the doll happens to the person as well (although, in real life, only good things like healing are done by ethical voodoo practitioners to the people the dolls represent). That is another example of a sympathetic link between two items.

In a magical ritual, almost anything can be used to establish a sympathetic link in the mind of the magician. Seeds can be used to represent fertility, a weapon can be used to symbolize protection, and blood can be used to symbolize life, or the life of a particular person, which is the other use of blood in magic. However, there seems to be two different types of sympathetic links: mental links; and "magnetic" ones (the word "magnetic" is in quotes because it refers to an occult attraction, and not to physical magnetism).

Mental links are the most commonly used or encountered ones. That is when the association of some object with an idea is made in the mind of the magician. His or her mental powers then make the magical goal materialize in some way. Mental links cannot be made without the intentional, or sometimes unintentional, efforts of a person.

"Magnetic" links, on the other hand, have nothing to do with the belief of an individual. Once they are established, they are real to anyone who comes into contact with them. For example, certain herbs affect individuals in ways that science cannot yet explain, whether they are burned as incense or taken internally. There is probably some "magnetic" connection between those herbs and the effects they have on people (healing, etc.) that was established naturally, without human intervention. Such a link might naturally exist between blood and lifeforce or vitality.

If the concept of that link is accepted, it becomes easy to imagine that a magically animated body could be sustained by blood. That would apply to our previously mentioned theory that a vampire might be a demonically animated corpse; the demon would use the energy in the blood to maintain the new vampire body. The power of blood can also apply to other theories if we accept that an immortal blood-drinking vampire is a corpse that is somehow animated and feeds off others to survive. As we shall see later, psychic vampires survive off that same energy, although they do not need the medium of blood to acquire it.

Another possible cause of vampirism is the one that is oftgen used in fiction. That is when a person is either attacked by a vampire and consequently becomes one, or when a person is given the blood of a vampire to become one. Both of those causes are also found in folklore, although what would be the occult significance behind either? Also, if that is how vampires are created, who created the first vampire?

As for the first question, if there were an immortal blood drinker in the world, then its blood would be infused with its immortal lifeforce just as a mortal's is fused with mortal lifeforce. By attacking a mortal, the vampire could possibly mix some of its lifeforce with the mortal's just by coming into contact with the open wound it makes. The principles at work in "magnetism" and sympathetic magic would be the same ones that give a vampire's victim a chance of becoming undead as well. Those principles would be even stronger if a vampire were to offer its blood to a person to drink, or if it were to force someone into the act.

Now for the origin of the first vampire. If the transfer of blood is a way that vampires can be created, it does not necessarily mean that it is the only way. The possible cause of vampirism we looked at earlier (demonic possession) along with the ones that follow might seem a little unlikely, but it would have to have occurred only once. From then on, the giving of the "magnetized" blood would be the only thing necessary to continue a line of vampires into eternity. Maybe the different species of vampires in the world are nothing more than creatures who were created by different "first" vampires. Any differences between the species could be the result of the different ways each "first" vampire was created.

We've already seen mention in folklore of how those who suffer a violent death are likely to become vampires. An occult explanation of that depends upon a belief in the soul surviving bodily death. If that soul still has memories of its earthly life, then it would also have memories of how it died. Therefore, if a soul felt that it shouldn't have died in a certain manner, it would probably not be able to find peace in the afterlife. As a result, the soul might become bound to the earth. The explanation of what could happen as a result also applies to the next theory, so we'll deal with it in a moment.

Another way a soul could become bound to the earth is if it is so evil that at death it fears moving on. A soul like that might be afraid there is nowhere for it to go. It would therefore cling to the earth using its willpower.

Both of the preceding types of bound souls would be "magnetically" attracted to their corpses. If the will of such a soul were strong enough, it might be able to infuse the body with some degree of "life." Then, if blood really does contain the lifeforce that occultists believe it does, the animated body would probably sense that lifeforce and instinctively hunt down humans to maintain its own existence, possibly creating more vampires. There is a similar principle at work in cases of psychic vampirism (as dealt with later in this book).

Another possible occult cause that should be mentioned also has its parallel in cases of psychic vampirism. That is the idea that an evil magician can become a vampire at death. In the case of immortal blood drinkers, that would probably happen in one of two ways: either the magician would make a pact with some demonic entity that could make it a vampire, or the magician might learn a magical technique for animating his or her body after death. Both seem improbable, but they are just variations of the causes we've already examined.

The last cause we'll examine is one I've mentioned in a few places already—excommunication. Like the previous cause, the occult principles at work have already been partially explained. When a person is excommunicated, he or she is ritualistically cursed by a priest. If the person is a believer in a certain faith, then his or her own belief would make the curse valid (and even if curse is pronounced after death, because there would be a "magnetic" link established to the soul through the excommunication ritual).

The curse pronounced basically states that the soul may never find peace and could never be a part of God's kingdom. Some bishops or priests used to add the following line at the end of an excommunication: "After death, let not thy body have power to dissolve." That, combined with the belief that "whatsoever is bound on earth shall be bound in heaven," would mean that a soul or individual (depending upon when the curse was pronounced) who believed in the potency of that curse would most likely become bound to the earth. If that happens, then it, too, could become a vampire (like the other types of earth-bound souls already discussed).

An excommunicated soul would also probably have a strong hatred driving the reanimation of its corpse. It can only be imagined what kind of fierce vampire would be the result of such a reanimation.

Of course, the belief of the person who is excommunicated might not be the only power at work when the ritual is performed. There are many reported incidents of excommunicated corpses that did not decompose until an absolution prayer was read over them. Perhaps there really is occult power at work in excommunication. Whether it works due to belief or power of its own, it does seem possible that it works on some level.

We have examined the cases of some ferocious vampires in this chapter—deadly creatures that preyed upon the blood of others. As we shall see in the next chapter, not all bloodthirsty vampires are undead. The mortal blood drinkers of the past have proven to be equally ferocious, and responsible for just as many deaths as their seemingly immortal counterparts.

Chapter Four

Mortal Blood Drinkers of the Past

D racula. The name has become synonymous with vampirism in the past century thanks to Bram Stoker's 1897 novel of the same name and Bela Lugosi's portrayal of the character on the screen. Of course, the Dracula of the silver screen does not closely resemble the literary Dracula. Whoever reads the novel after seeing any of the hundreds of images of vampires that fill stores every Halloween is likely to be quite shocked.

Lugosi's Dracula, a portrayal that has been copied again and again, was a sophisticated-looking monster dressed in a tuxedo and cape. Stoker's Dracula never wore a cape (the cape was an invention of Hamilton Deane, who adapted Dracula as a play). Lugosi was considered by many to be a very handsome vampire, which is another contrast to the literary Dracula, who was an almost animal-like creature with ears that were "at the tops extremely pointed," hairy palms, and sharp nails.

There are, of course, differences between other actors who played Dracula and the literary count in Stoker's novel, but those variations between print and film are not the end of our Dracula comparison. It seems that there are also a few differences between Stoker's Dracula and, as you might have guessed, the real Dracula.

Who was the man who inspired the world's most famous literary monster? According to those who wrote about the real Dracula's endless atrocities, he was a monster as well. In fact, as we shall see, Vlad Dracula committed many acts that rival the literary Dracula when it comes to cruelty. However, why did Stoker turn him into a vampire in his novel? Was Dracula a vampire?

The creatures described in the pages that follow possessed no supernatural powers, yet still thrived off the blood of others. They are the mortal blood drinkers of the past—humans who earned the title of "monster" or "vampire" because of their unexplainable bloodlust. The next chapter will deal with the modern incarnation of these creatures; vampires who, for the most part, do not take blood without permission. For now, prepare yourself for a look at some terrifying mortals who have proven, in some cases concretely, that their category of vampire exists.

Of course, there might not at first glance seem to be anything occult about these individuals, but upon closer examination it becomes clear that there actually is something very occult (hidden) about them: their motives. Why would humans want to drink the blood of others? In modern times, the answer to that could simply be that they want to imitate what they read about in fiction or see on the screen. In the next chapter, we will look at some of those modern, mortal blood drinkers who have written to me, telling their stories. That will make it possible to determine at least some of their motivations. In fact, some of those letters are from vampires claiming to be true immortals, which, if untrue, tells us a lot about their motivation (again, the influence of fiction).

What about the individuals described in the sections that follow? We could look at their acts and wonder, or we could take their actions as possible signs that they instinctively felt the power and lifeforce in blood that could possibly keep an immortal blood drinker "alive." Perhaps the types of individuals described below were evil enough to make them akin to the types of people described in the last chapter; the ones who cannot move on because of fear of the consequences of their actions. No matter what their motivations were, the mortal blood drinkers of the past set "the stage" for our examination of the same type of vampire in the present day.

With the exception of Prince Vlad Dracula, who eventually became a hero in the eyes of his subjects, the vampires in this chapter were all considered criminals, and met with terrible ends as a result. As a final comment on the motivations of these vampires, you will notice for yourself when you read the next chapter just how different the monsters that follow were from the people who consider themselves modern vampires.

The first two individuals we will examine have been associated with vampirism due to fictional and factual accounts. They were not as vampiric as the blood drinkers who are described later in this chapter, but are still included because they are the most famous mortals ever associated with vampirism.

Vlad Dracula

Vlad Dracula was born around the year 1431 in Sighisoara, Transylvania. His father was Vlad Dracul, which meant "Vlad the Dragon." He was given that name because he was in the Order of the Dragon, a group of soldiers who protected Christianity and the land of Eastern Europe from the Turks (Muslims). The suffix "a" added to "Dracul" means "son of," so the name "Dracula" meant "son of the Dragon." Dracula was eventually known by another name, but more on that later.

Dracula spent the earliest years of his adolescent life in his father's court. He was most likely trained in various physical disciplines and was taught to endure severe hardships that all future rulers must be able to endure. The throne of Wallachia, which would one day be his father's, would also eventually be Dracula's, and his father must have wanted his son to be prepared. The discipline was not necessary; Dracula had apparently been born with a strong mindset of his own.

From when he was very young, Dracula supposedly enjoyed watching criminals being taken from their cells to the courtyard to be executed (usually by hanging). That sadistic tendency was probably amplified when, at a young age, Dracula and his brother Radu were kept as hostages by the Turks to guarantee that Dracul would keep a pact he made with the Turkish Sultan. One can only imagine how cruelly he was treated and how he would have been affected by the treatment.

We will not get into the historical details of how Dracula eventually became ruler of Wallachia, as that part of his life takes us out of the scope of this chapter (for a detailed look at Dracula's life, see *Dracula: Prince of Many Faces* by Radu R. Florescu and Raymond T. McNally, which is listed in the Bibliography). Instead, let's look at his cruel behavior, which Stoker uncovered when researching Romanian legends.

Dracula was a sadistic ruler. Under his reign, crime eventually became non-existent because the punishment for any crime was death, usually by impalement, which took different forms. Normally, a tall, sharp, wooden stake was placed firmly into the ground. Criminals were then thrown on top of it, with their abdomens or backs facing the point, and were left there, their weight and the sharp points doing the rest. Another variation of the execution method included placing the victim vertically on the stake and having it enter through his or her rectum.

Dracula punished his subjects in other ways as well, but impalement was generally his preferred form of execution, and for that reason he was called Vlad Tepes, which means "Vlad the Impaler." He still preferred to call himself Dracula, however.

But what about blood drinking? Even though Romanian tales of Dracula do not label him a vampire, Radu R. Florescu and Raymond T. McNally have found mention of Dracula drinking the blood of his victims. Dracula often had dinner while he watched the executions he had ordered, and on one documented occasion, he included the blood of one of the executed in his meal (it is believed that he dipped his bread into it). However, there is not enough available evidence to show that he drank blood at any other time in his life.

If Dracula really did drink blood, it might have been to show his ultimate power over his subjects. Because of the lack of other evidence, Dracula is the least likely candidate for a true mortal blood drinker. Unlike some of those whose descriptions follow, Dracula did not seem to thrive on the act of drinking blood, but rather on its shedding. He is included in this chapter to show how Stoker's model for a fictional vampire actually did drink blood, at least once. However, Dracula provides another mystery that warrants his inclusion in this book.

Stoker said in his novel (through the medium of Dr. Van Helsing) that Dracula possessed such willpower that, combined with the strange occult forces of the land from which he came, he was able to return from the dead as a vampire. That willpower, Stoker mentions, certainly was a trait of the real Prince Dracula, and as for returning from the dead, there is a mystery surrounding Vlad Dracula's death and burial.

Dracula was supposedly assassinated and beheaded in 1476, probably by one of his political enemies. His corpse was then said to have been buried in the island Monastery of Snagov at the foot of the chapel altar. When that "grave" was opened during the course of diggings in 1931–32, it was found to contain some animal bones and a few artifacts. In another part of the monastery, a grave with a headless body was found, and the rotted clothes do seem to match those of a prince. Was Dracula's corpse moved? Was the headless body found in the other grave buried to throw Dracula's enemies off? We'll never know, although I'm sure that more than one fan of vampire fiction would like to believe that Dracula had really risen from the grave. Of course, if he did rise, then he should have been included in the last chapter, right?

The Blood Countess

Elizabeth Bathory, known as the Blood Countess, was a mortal blood drinker who has also been immortalized in literature and film, although rarely accurately. Bathory was born in Transylvania in 1560, and lived there until she married the Slovak Count Ferenc Nadasdy in 1575. The couple then lived in Nadasdy's castle in the Slovak Republic.

While heading her household, the always-cruel Countess began to punish her servants in vicious ways. Eventually, she began to kill some of them. Her husband died in 1604 (she was never implicated in his death), and Bathory apparently kept on murdering until suspicion about her activities arose in 1610. By that time, approximately 650 victims were said to have died at her hands. But what did she do with them?

In 1611, Bathory was convicted for her crimes and sentenced to life imprisonment in a room in her castle with no windows. Only a small hole was made for food and water to be passed to her. She died in that room three years later. Just as she was locked away, so were the records of what she had done. A Royal Edict declared that she was not even to be mentioned.

Years later, documents surfaced that detailed what Bathory had done, and helped her earn the title of "Blood Countess." Raymond T. McNally, one of the authors of *Dracula: Prince of Many Faces*, wrote a book about Bathory entitled *Dracula Was a Woman: In Search of the Blood Countess of Transylvania*. The title refers to the possibility that Bathory influenced Stoker's placement of the novel in Transylvania, even though Bathory started committing her crimes after she moved away from that district. More importantly, the book is valuable because it contains some of the legends that arose about Bathory's practices.

The most famous of those is the belief that the countess killed young ladies to bathe in their blood. She supposedly did that to become younger. In one instance, a girl accused Bathory of biting her. That method of attack, along with the bathing in blood, has sparked interest in the countess and has surrounded her with vampiric legends. However, like Dracula, it can't be proven whether the countess felt the urge to drink the blood of her victims.

It has been speculated that evidence and testimony in the Bathory trial was kept from the public. More than one writer has assumed that some of those lost records include descriptions of various acts of vampirism that Bathory might have performed. Of particular note is Gabriel Ronay, who McNally cites as having said that Bathory's "acts of vampirism and ritual murder were kept out of the trial records."

Let's say for a moment that the Blood Countess did not actually drink her victims' blood, and only bathed in it, apparently with the intent of appearing younger (Stoker used the idea of growing younger with the help of blood in his novel, although his fictional count drank it to accomplish that). What would make Bathory believe that doing so would make her appear younger? McNally includes a particularly interesting translation from the German scholar Michael Wagener in his book that shows how Bathory could have come to think the way she did. Here's an excerpt:

> *Elizabeth used to dress up well in order to please her husband.... On one occasion, her chambermaid saw something wrong with her headdress, and as a recompense for observing it, received such a severe box on the ear that blood gushed from her nose and spurted on her mistress's face.... When the blood drops were washed off her face, her skin appeared more beautiful: whiter and more transparent on the spots where the blood had been. Elizabeth, therefore, formed the resolve to bathe her face and her entire body in human blood, so as to enhance her beauty....*

The account goes on to mention details of how Bathory, with the help of her assistants, would kill her victims and bathe in their blood at four in the morning. Is that account accurate? Even if only the first couple of lines are true, we know that the countess was a person who obviously took her appearance very seriously and could act viciously when it came to matters concerning it. As for whether the skin of the countess became "whiter and more transparent" after being splashed with blood, I'm sure many medical professionals would disagree. It seems that in her rage, the countess had delusions she didn't want to surrender at a later time. If she was as cruel a person as historians claim, the "rejuvenating" bloodbaths might have been a convenient excuse to her subconscious for her behavior.

Until the late nineteenth century, investigations of the activities of mortal blood drinkers were usually surrounded with a great deal of superstition, making it difficult to tell exactly what really happened. In other words, ridiculous accusations were made about the status of the blood drinkers' souls, and not enough factual evidence was compiled about the crimes they committed.

The following case is a good example. It is a little short, due to the lack of accurate information available, but it illustrates how easily facts can become distorted or even invented in courts of the past.

Gilles de Rais

Born in 1404, Gilles de Rais grew up to become a great soldier of the French Army; it has been written that he and Joan of Arc shared the battlefield against the English. In addition to his military fame, Gilles was quite wealthy, and of the upper class. Finally, he was considered a bloodthirsty killer.

Gilles was arrested and brought to trial on the accusation that he was responsible for the rising number of missing boys from the area. According to his peers and his own admission, Gilles was involved in researching and practicing magic and alchemy, which was not unusual, as several wealthy individuals of that era delved into the arcane arts. It is not certain, however, whether those acts made him a suspicious individual in the eyes of his peers or if hard evidence existed to support his arrest. It is possible that Gilles' peers simply feared the occult.

As was common in those days, Gilles was tortured during the trial in hopes of obtaining a confession. His torturers were not disappointed. Gilles admitted to torturing the young boys, drinking their blood, and murdering them. That hysterical confession and the amount of self-incriminating information it supposedly contained, with the sensational associations between Gilles' alleged crimes and his occult interests, make it difficult to tell what really happened. Just how much of Gilles confession was coaxed out of him, as was done in the witch trials?

The occult practices of de Rais have been referred to as Satanic. If he did practice evil magic, it is even more likely that he could have performed the acts he admitted, making de Rais a "monster" the likes of which hasn't been seen often in history. Gilles was found guilty and executed in 1440. His remains were burned.

Now let's turn our attention to a few more-recent vampires. There is a great deal of evidence available to support the factual nature of the actions of these mortal blood drinkers, due to the efficiency of the legal system in effect during the cases. When the vampires were "hunted," no evidence or testimony was hidden. The vampire hunters in the following cases used notebooks in addition to badges, handcuffs, and guns.

We can assume that the law enforcement agents who hunted the following vampires knew they were after mortals, so the abundance of information just mentioned should not seem out of the ordinary. However, as you read the cases, try to imagine what the investigators would have done if they had reason to believe that the vampires they were hunting were not human. Would cases of immortal blood drinkers receive the same publicity as the following ones, or would they be kept secret?

Fritz Haarman

Born in Germany in 1879, Fritz Haarman was another military man turned vampire. He was the sixth child in an impoverished family, and openly showed his hatred for his father from a young age. Haarman was a disturbed child, and his condition worsened as he approached his teen years. At the age of seventeen, he was arrested for child molesting and was put in a mental institution. He escaped soon after and made his way back home, where he became engaged to a young lady who became pregnant with his child. When the baby was stillborn, Haarman called off the wedding plans and left to join the army.

For someone as disturbed as Haarman, it is surprising that he did well in the military. He probably would have remained in the army were it not for medical problems. Haarman was diagnosed as having neurasthenia and was discharged in 1903. Desperate, Haarman changed his lifestyle to the complete opposite of what it was in the military. He went from his brief period of following orders and being disciplined, to breaking laws and being a criminal. He was caught and arrested often for minor offenses, and spent a good portion of the next decade in prison.

Sometime around 1917 or 1918, Haarman met a male prostitute named Hans Grans, who would become his partner in some sadistic and vampiric crimes. Haarman and Grans would bring young men to their home and feed them a filling dinner, with plenty of alcohol to wash it down. Then, when a victim became tired from all the food and alcohol, Haarman would seize him and bite into his neck, sucking on his blood until the helpless victim died.

It is estimated that Haarman vampirized some fifty young men, although he was only accused of killing twenty-seven. What did he and Grans do with all of those bodies? The answer to that is pretty gruesome—they chopped the bodies into steaks and sold them on the streets as beef. That "underground" meat market went on from 1918 to 1924.

Of course, the complete bodies of the victims could not be turned into sellable meats. Grans and Haarman dumped the bones and organs into a canal. That would eventually become their undoing; bones and skulls floated to the surface in 1924. The police were already suspicious of Haarman because of his history, and went to question him about the cases of missing men from the area during the past six years.

They found more than enough evidence to connect Haarman to the victims—their clothes were still in his house. Haarman eventually confessed to the crimes and became known as the "Vampire of Hanover." He was sentenced to death, and, at his own request, was decapitated in a public execution in December of 1924. Hans Grans would go on to serve only twelve years in jail.

The evidence in the case of Franz Haarman is complete enough to show us that he was truly a disturbed individual. What is not known is whether he was imitating fictional vampires when he attacked his victims in the manner described, or whether he was simply acting on some monstrous instinct. We will explore more deeply in the next chapter different motivations that are the keys to understanding why mortal blood drinkers exist.

Now let's move on to another early twentieth-century vampire who has achieved notoriety for his grisly actions.

John Haigh

John Haigh (date of birth uncertain) was raised by a devout puritanical family in Yorkshire, England. As a result, he was a very religious child, and was even a choir boy. From the information that has been gathered, it is clear that Haigh was well liked by all who knew him when he was young. When he moved out to live on his own, however, he changed.

This vampire's career of evil began, like that of Haarman's, in a non-vampiric way. John Haigh spent several years of his adult life serving time for thefts. We can't be sure how those years affected Haigh; however, when he finally got out of prison, he was anything but a common thief. He stole more than just his victims' possessions; he also took their blood.

In 1943, Haigh was released from prison for the last time before performing the crimes that made him famous as a mortal blood drinker. After he got out, he murdered a young man by the name of Donald McSwann. Haigh then proceeded to drink the man's blood, take some of his belongings, and dissolve the body in sulfuric acid, apparently believing that there would be no evidence with which to convict him.

That gruesome modus operandi would be the one that Haigh would follow for approximately five years. In that time, John Haigh murdered and drank the blood of McSwann's parents, along with three other individuals, disposing of their bodies each time in acid. You might be wondering by now how we know that Haigh drank his victims' blood if all of their bodies were dissolved? Like Haarman, when Haigh was caught, he confessed.

The vampiric killer's last victim was a wealthy woman named Mrs. Durand-Deacon. Haigh fooled her into thinking they could go into the artificial fingernail business together. When she went to his home to see the materials for the undertaking, Haigh shot her in the back of the head. He told police that he then went to his car, got a drinking glass, and returned to the corpse. Using what he said might have been a pen knife, Haigh cut into the side of the woman's neck and filled his glass with her blood. After he drank, he took all of his victim's valuables and dissolved her body, or so he thought.

Parts of Haigh's last victim did not dissolve. Among the remains were bones, dentures, and part of a foot that helped to positively identify the victim as the missing Mrs. Durand-Deacon. This evidence led Haigh to testify to all the previously mentioned acts. He was hanged for his crimes in 1949.

The preceding mortals all had some form of "need" for blood that translated into violent actions. As explained earlier, there really is nothing supernatural about mortal blood drinkers, and for that reason, most feel they are the only beings who ever deserved the title of vampire. You might have noticed that I do not agree with those feelings.

The real importance of the vampires in this chapter, and their less violent counterparts described in the next one, is that they show the potential for the predatory nature in humans, both living and dead. Vicious individuals who prey on others while alive might not cease doing so after death. Some occult force or condition, such as the ones explained earlier (and later on), would have to be met for that to happen, but isn't the possibility made easier to accept by the existence of mortal blood drinkers?

Before making up your mind as to whether these individuals could be responsible for the existence of other types of vampires, take the opportunity to get into some of their minds and find out what they're thinking. The next chapter contains some of their stories in their own words. A few of them claim to be "more" than just regular humans, for a variety of reasons. You can decide that for yourself as well.

Chapter Five

Mortal Blood Drinkers
of the Present Day

We are real, we are many, we are forever....
—An Anonymous Vampire

P repare yourself for something a little different. So far, we have let the reports of vampire victims and hunters (including those who are police) relate information about the activities of blood drinkers. In this chapter, we'll let some of them speak for themselves, or actually, write for themselves, in the form of letters.

The preliminary research for this book began in 1993 when I helped some victims of psychic vampirism (those cases are related in later chapters). Those experiences helped me to see that there definitely were other types of vampires in the world besides the type popular fiction portrays.

My search for those other types led me to an organization known as the Vampire Information Exchange, which publishes the VIE newsletter, or *VIEN*. I found that several people who were members of that organization claimed to be living vampires. By placing an ad in the *VIEN*, I got some of them to write me letters describing themselves and their vampiric lifestyles for possible inclusion in this book.

As I began to receive letters, I noticed that many of them were imitations of the lives of famous fictional vampires (none of those letters are printed here). I was forming various theories in my mind at that time about why the letter writers claimed to be who they were. One of those theories (that most would probably agree with) is that the letter writers were just people who liked vampire fiction, and wanted to imitate it. For that reason, I decided to also place an ad in a popular magazine for horror and vampire fans: *Fangoria*.

Those two ads pulled in the letters that were selected for inclusion here. The ones from *Fangoria* were "keyed" so that I would be able to tell them apart from the others. Interestingly enough, the more supernatural letters came from that magazine. In fact, a lot of those letters were from vampires who believed they were immortal. I decided to include only two of those letters from "immortals" (in this chapter on mortal vampires) because they contained some unique ideas.

In total, I received eighty-two letters. Aside from space limitations, there are a few reasons many of them were not included here. First of all, many of the letters from "immortals" contained obvious historical errors that made it clear the vampires who wrote them were not born when they said they were. Those same letters often contained numerous errors in grammar and spelling—it's hard to imagine someone living for eight centuries and not learning how to spell simple words. Apparently, quite a few vampires hunt "pray" at night and remain "doormint" during the day.

Second, letters that were nothing more than a paragraph of "power raving" were not included. If the letter said little more than "you are all helpless" or "we shall rule the world," it does not appear here.

Interestingly, the preceding considerations almost completely eliminated from consideration the letters from "immortals." Therefore, this chapter on mortal blood drinkers (with the inclusion of two "supernatural" beings) took form. A final consideration was whether the letter writer included permission to publish the letter. Unfortunately, some interesting letters could not be published because permission was not given, and neither was an address so that I could obtain that permission.

In some cases, permission to publish the letters was given under the condition that the writers would remain anonymous. That was an easy enough request to oblige. All of the letters that follow contain either a pseudonym that was provided by the letter writer or a simplified version of that name provided by myself. No real first-and-last-name combinations are given, although some real first names or first and last initials are given.

Let's get back to the theories I developed as to why the letter writers claim to be vampires. I mentioned that many of them seemed to be imitating fictional vampires. Whether they actually live the way they claim is another matter. Either way, they are probably not blood drinkers for any reason other than they like what they have seen or read.

Some of the letters contain what appear to be original lifestyles and stories. Of course, that does not rule out those individuals as vampires who were influenced by fiction. Despite what they write, it is possible that most mortal blood drinkers of the present day do what they do because they think it is "cool" to be like Dracula or Lestat.

Besides the need to imitate fictional vampires, two other explanations as to why there are mortal blood drinkers are possible: they were either born with some psychological need to drink blood, or there is actually some supernatural reason why they "thrive" on the substance.

As for the psychological need, I have learned of a disorder often referred to as "Renfield's Syndrome." The presence of that disease becomes evident in a person from a very young age. A child with the disorder is often caught drinking blood from a wound on either him or herself or on a playmate. The disorder progresses so that by the time the individual becomes an adult, he or she might go so far as to break into a blood bank to get the needed sustenance.

There are a couple of things that separate people with Renfield's Syndrome from those who simply like to pretend to be vampires. First, those with the syndrome do not necessarily claim to like the night or darkness, or to fear the sun for any reason (many of the mortal blood drinkers in this chapter curiously have several attributes that make them similar to fictional vampires). Second, those with the disorder could not possibly be imitating fictional characters because they began drinking blood at very young ages—not many four-year-olds are vampire fanatics who want to imitate their idols.

Finally, let's look at the possibility that mortal blood drinkers are the way they are for some supernatural reason. The vampires in this chapter all claim there is something very real inside them that makes them need blood. Some even feel that the drinking of blood, on some esoteric level, is absolutely essential to their survival (one vampire, Dante, gives a few interesting occult theories of his own as to why he needs blood). However, it is difficult to determine from letters whether that is true.

Whatever the motivations behind them might be, I hope the letters I have selected help shed some light on this dark subculture. As with all the information presented in this book, please read it and feel free to make up your own mind.

Note: The following letters do not address a problem with the practice of blood drinking: the possibility of spreading disease, particularly AIDS. That serious problem will be examined in the next chapter. The author felt it important to make it clear at this point that the practices described in the following pages are potentially dangerous.

A Different Kind of Renfield

We'll start with this short letter from a vampire who claims to have something in common with the character Renfield in Dracula. However, as you shall see, he is not necessarily someone who has Renfield's Syndrome.

The character Renfield, whose name has been mentioned several times already, was a lunatic in the novel Dracula who believed that it was possible to become immortal by gathering accumulated "life" from lower creatures. By feeding flies to spiders, then those spiders to birds, then eating the birds himself, Renfield felt that he was absorbing all that accumulation of strong life into himself. In the character's mind, that would make him worthy in the eyes of "the master," Dracula, to be given the gift of eternal life. It should be clear to the reader how the following letter shows the writer's obvious inspiration from that story.

> *I would like to tell you of my vampiric lifestyle. You may print this letter under the condition that you do not reveal my true identity in your book. Where I live, word travels quickly and I would most probably be ridiculed and forced out of town. For that reason, you can call me the Vampire Jeremy.*
>
> *Why do I consider myself to be a vampire—a predator? I kill animals and drink their blood, that's why. Don't*

confuse me with the types of so-called vampires that you hear about today. They do not impress me. They do not hunt their prey, but only stick hypodermic needles into themselves to trade blood. They are not hunters.

To obtain my sustenance I mainly kill mammals, but I will also drink the cold blood of reptiles. I suppose that my drinking from lower creatures than humans makes me a little like the character "Renfield" from the novel Dracula. *But I am not insane.*

I wait for immortality and drink of the lower creatures until a noble undead will one day take me as his or her own. I wait and believe that night will come, and have prepared for it.

Because of the lack of details we have about Jeremy's childhood, it would be difficult to determine what started this vampire on his way. However, Jeremy does give us a major clue in his last couple of lines: By saying that he is waiting for a "noble undead" to come and take him, he has given a pretty good indication that fiction and not gut instinct motivates his actions.

An Ethical Vampire?

As a few letters in this chapter will show, not all vampires in the world are ruthless individuals. Some of them claim to be basically "good people" who are just a little different. A few even have pronounced spiritual beliefs that make it hard to believe they could possibly identify themselves with creatures of darkness. Here's the first letter I received from a vampire who is interested in positive metaphysics and morality.

Hello, my name is Vampiress Paulina. I am not a sexdriven vampire or a violent vampire, and I'm completely sane. I drink blood because it is my natural instinct and

*need; I believe I was born to become a vampire. That ties
in with my belief in reincarnation and that my soul is
very old. Unlike what you would expect from a vampire,
I strive for enlightenment and spirituality.*

*The life of a vampire is intoxicating, but it can also be
a lonely existence. Even as a child, I was fascinated with
the dark side of life, and was drawn to it. In school I
never really "fit in" with the crowd. I had only a few
friends, and I've always been a loner. Sadly, my parents
can never truly know me. My family believes I'm a little
bit eccentric, and that I'm fascinated with vampirism,
but that that's as far as it goes. They are quite wrong.*

*I always had a tendency to bite, but I didn't really
understand why until I grew older. I could feel a powerful energy building inside of me, and I just knew it was
blood I hungered for. I believe it was my fate to become
a vampire. I went through a difficult period when I felt
like I was going mad by my vampiric way of thinking. I
had a hard time accepting the fact that I was indeed a
vampire, because of the beliefs and morals my parents
instilled in me. On the other hand, I knew I had to be
true to myself. The madness ended when I accepted being
a vampire, and my true self was finally able to emerge.*

*Being a vampire doesn't make me an evil person. I
would never intentionally hurt another individual to get
blood, or for any other reason, as a matter of fact.
Rather, I have found donors who let me take blood from
them in a number of ways. When they don't wish to be
bitten by me, I use a sterile lancet. Only a few drops
come out from such a small wound, but it's enough to
satisfy me, and it spares them a lot of pain.*

*We vampires are not necessarily bad people, and I
would like others to know that. You may print this letter
for that reason.*

It is worth pointing out what Paulina says about how she obtains her blood. Many mortal blood drinkers claim to drink only from "donors" who let the vampires feed from them, in both painful and painless ways. (For those who don't know, the sterile lancets Paulina mentions are small metal needles that are usually used by diabetics to test their blood at home.)

A Blood-Drinking, Working Mother

Here's a letter writer who feels that her vampiric nature gives her certain enhanced abilities. As we shall soon see, she is not alone in that claim of vampiric superiority. She is also a single parent, and her story is made more interesting by the fact that she feels her boys might be taking after her!

I have been a vampire for a long time, although I never really knew it until recently when I learned that there are others like me in the world, and it seems they are giving interviews on television! I feel that I would like to share my story as well, so here goes.

I am a night person. If I could, I would sleep until dusk and stay up until dawn. But seeing how I have three children, and a day job, that can't work. In order for me to sleep at night, I have to take a prescription sleeping pill. Otherwise, something in my body clicks around 9:00 PM and I'm on the go. My two sons seem to be this way, too. I sometimes think that vampirism is hereditary, but if it is, why didn't my daughter get it? I'm really not sure.

My senses are heightened; I have a keen sense of hearing and smell. I always wear sunglasses during the day (even in winter)—the light hurts my eyes. I also have a strong sixth sense, what many would call E.S.P. Sometimes I can tell what is going to happen in a situation before it does. I can also tell what people are thinking or feeling on occasion. But those are only minor traits.

My hunger for blood grows every day. I'm not able to satisfy my need, so I must continually look for a donor. Alas, no luck. When I can no longer stand the hunger, I often cut myself in an inconspicuous spot and drink. It hardly satisfies me, though. I long to find a willing partner who I can fully experience blood drinking with, on a regular basis—it is really an incredible feeling. When I do drink, it gives me first a sense of peace, then of control, and finally of power and energy.

Before I go any further, let me make it clear that I don't take drugs. I do drink occasionally (about once every two weeks), but so do most people. I consider myself a "normal" working mother (during the day, that is). Although I might dress a little odd as far as most people are concerned (all my clothes are black or have black in them).

I'm constantly obtaining and searching for new information on vampires. I love my vampire nature so much that I had a red-lipped mouth with fangs and blood dripping tattooed on my left breast. My diet consists of red meat prepared raw to rare. Otherwise, it is normal— fruits, veggies, etc.

I'm not into any organized religion, but constantly seek information on Wicca and ritualistic magic. You have my permission to use any of the information in this letter that you need. However, please use only my first name: Tracy.

That last part about how Tracy is looking for information on Wicca and ritualistic magic might seem a bit out of place but, actually, many of the letters I received were from people who were interested in some form of occultism or magic. The next letter is another example.

Prepared to Meet an Immortal

Here is another vampire who has some non-vampiric occult interests as well. Like Jeremy, she claims to be ready for an immortal to come and take her, and even tries to establish communication with other vampires using her Ouija board. Of all the letters, this one perhaps provides the greatest insight into what might have caused its writer to search for an eccentric outlet in life, at a young age.

My name is Megan. I am in my early twenties and I live with my boyfriend. On the outside that might make me seem like a lot of other people, but inside I've always thought that I am different from others. So, when I started to drink blood a couple of months ago, it seemed natural for me to do so.

I had a fairly normal childhood, and I was really close to my dad. He was killed by a drunk driver when I was 13, and his death affected me greatly, but by the age of 16, I was pretty much over the pain. It was around that time that I started to take a serious interest in vampires. Before then, I believed in them, but I had never read any vampire books. The first one that I read was Interview With the Vampire *by Anne Rice, and I thought at that time that it was the greatest thing ever written.*

Also around that time, I started to dress in black every time I went out, including to school. I had the need to dress differently from others because I knew that there was something weird about me. I always thought morbid thoughts and had different opinions on subjects than the masses. It was after high school that I started to collect books about vampires, fact and fiction. I was hungry to read about documented cases, but they are very difficult to find.

Not until I met my current boyfriend did I tell any-body that I believed in vampires. My mother actually thought I was a satanist for a while because of the music groups that I listen to, such as the Misfits, Danzig, and Christian Death; however, I do not believe in the devil. When I moved in with my boyfriend, we created a vam-pire shrine where I keep my vampire books, occult objects, and Dracula items. My occult items have to do with the Wiccan belief (a positive, Earth religion), not devil worship.

It was back in late 1992 that I first drank my own blood; I did it for no reason other than I was drawn to the thought of tasting blood. I was just sitting in the bed-room of the house my boyfriend and I shared before we moved to our current place, and I had the urge to cut my arm. It was like an outside force made me do it, but I am not saying that I didn't enjoy it. When I first tasted it, the feeling that I received can only be compared to sex. That really surprised me, because I never really consid-ered myself a sexual person.

Since that first time, I drank my blood only when I felt the compelling urge to do so. My boyfriend let me drink from him once, but I hate having to cut him. He doesn't mind, but I feel guilty just the same! What I'd really like to find is another girl my age to exchange blood with. I think that if I had the chance to do this with somebody that held the exact beliefs as myself, it would be a more fulfilling experience. Also, I would feel safest with another girl.

I know for a fact that I do not have a blood fetish. When I drink blood, I do so for my body. Even though it gives me a natural high that feels as good as sex, it does not make me feel like having sex. Actually, the need I feel for blood goes beyond a physical nature. If I don't drink blood and if my mind is telling me to do so, I feel manic and the slightest thing will get me in a bad mood.

When I went to play miniature golf last week, I got burned really badly on my upper arms. I had not had a sunburn since last summer, and I thought that it would go away just as fast as the others. Instead, my arms remained badly burned for twice as long, and I felt weaker than I ever had. For that reason, I don't like to go out in the sunlight that much.

I've never believed in the Christian symbols that represent God. Crosses and crucifixes mean nothing to me. However, I don't really feel comfortable going into churches because I don't believe in what they represent. As I mentioned earlier, I don't believe in the devil, either. I think organized religions are false and based on the fear of what God will do to you if you go against Him. I prefer the balanced and understanding deities of Wicca.

It really gets me angry when people say that individuals who believe in vampires or think that they themselves are vampires are crazy. I know that I am not crazy. In fact, I think I'm a pretty rational person. For that reason I'm afraid to call myself a vampire, but I guess I am a mortal one. I know that there are supernatural ones out there. Maybe what I am going through is but a transition stage to prepare me to meet a true vampire.

A few months ago, I contacted a "vampire" spirit through my Ouija board. I wrote to someone knowledgeable in the subject, and she warned me to be careful in the future. After that night, I actually drank blood three days in a row. I think that the spirit in the board influenced me to do so.

You can use any of that in your book. I hope you found some of my story helpful in understanding about mortal vampires.

I have to admit I was surprised at first to find vampires who are also interested in Wicca. Wiccans or Witches are people who practice (as Megan said) a "positive" religion. They fervently protest the harming of others, believing that whatever they do to others comes back to them three times as good or bad, as the case may be. Megan and many other vampires take blood only from those who are willing, but as we'll explore in the next chapter, blood drinking is dangerous and possibly deadly. It would be interesting to learn how other Witches feel about the practices of mortal blood drinkers.

A Reluctant Vampire

This vampire is uncertain about his vampire nature, and seems amost upset about being one. However, as he states in his letter, he seems to have picked up what he does subconsciously through reading books. That makes it a little difficult to comment on this letter any further, so it will be included and left to the reader to decide about the writer's authenticity.

> I really don't know where to start, but I guess the first place is, I'm an eighteen-year-old vampire. I can't exactly say how long I've been one for sure, but I know that it's been at least for as long as I can remember.
>
> Being a vampire is not something that is easy to deal with because of some of the "nutcases" out there today. Some might say that I am a nutcase as well, but I just consider myself to be a young guy trying to live a normal life, even though my instincts tell me to follow a different way of living. I drink blood.
>
> Some of my friends know about what I do. They know about it from reading the same books as I do, and by seeing me drink from a common friend. My parents don't know. I want it to stay that way, for I hope that in the

future I will change and no longer have this "need" for blood. I don't know if I need it to live. I don't think so; I just think it's a desire, like sex is for some people.

I would like to be in your book of course, only under the alias of SR. Thank you for giving me the chance to speak openly about what I feel is a horrible trait which has stricken me and many others in this world of ours.

Don't get me wrong. I do enjoy being a vampire, but sometimes I would just like to be like everyone else.

Dante and the Art of Vampyrcraeft

Of all the letters received from those claiming to be mortal blood drinkers, the letter that follows, from a writer who calls himself Dante, offers the most complete explanation as to how a mortal vampire could benefit from the act of drinking blood. What is fascinating about the letter is the theory as to why people in the past would have mistaken the attack of a mortal blood drinker for that of an immortal, folkloric or "mythic" vampire.

From an occult point of view, some of the ideas Dante presents in the pages that follow are feasible, although he does fail to explain just what makes someone a vampire. He provides explanations of powers (what he calls Vampyrcraeft) that can be attained by a vampire, but does not explain why any person couldn't attain those same abilities if he or she were also to drink blood.

Besides that minor criticism, Dante's letter deserves a close read. It provides an accurate, inside look at the mind of a vampire who seems to believe what he says is true. Remember, whatever his or her motivation might be, a mortal blood drinker is simply a mortal who drinks blood. The explanations of powers and characteristics that make a vampire "superior" in his or her own eyes could only be imagined (either consciously or subconsciously). Is that the case with Dante? You decide.

As a vampire, I, for obvious reasons, would prefer to remain anonymous. You may print this letter, but please refer to me only as Dante. I welcome this opportunity to explain what I am, but do not wish to reveal who I am.

It was common knowledge to the learned individuals of ancient times that existence consisted of three levels, or states, of being: the Physical World—the material realm of flesh and substance; the Mental Realm—the plane in which thoughts, ideas, and knowledge were stored, processed, and received from; and the Spiritual, or Astral, Domain—where emotions, self-will, intuition, faith, and the vital force of life resided. A person is the composite of all three of those states, and each form is anchored to the others by a series of links that serve to keep one whole. The brain links the Physical plane to the Mental plane as a transceiver and translator of raw thought energy. The subconscious links the Mental plane with the Spiritual one, creating a gate through which a dreamer could catch fleeting glimpses of the Astral realm during deep sleep. Finally, the Spirit is linked to the Physical through blood. The blood is the Life.

I believe that this is true, and that by drinking blood, and through it obtaining vital force, I can enhance my own spiritual energy. The state of the soul determines the condition of the body and mind. A healthy, well-fed spirit will allow the physique and psyche to remain in top form, for as long as fresh life-force is consumed. Humans lose their vital energy over time, their spirit thins, and this is reflected in their mind and body. Vampires, however, may reconstitute their spiritual force indefinitely through regular infusions of the life-force of others. That will maintain a healthy body, a sharp mind, and will slow the natural aging process. I, myself, am around 25 and am often mistaken for a young teenager.

The blood must be living for me to siphon the energy from it. Young children seem to have the strongest vitality, while animals have the weakest. I find that about a tablespoon of adult blood a week is enough to sate my needs and keep my spirit at peak vitality. However, blood is highly addictive to me, and I often purchase beef blood to drink for pleasure, though I receive nothing else from it.

If a vampire drinks more than is needed, the excess spiritual energy may be used to perform a number of extra-natural mental and physical abilities. Flight and transformations of any type are not possible to the best of my knowledge. The effects are usually more subtle, such as causing someone to not notice your presence although you are directly in their sight, manipulating the dreams of others, or obtaining sudden bursts of adrenal strength or speed. There are myriad others, but the specifics are not what are important here. What is important is that this excess vitality can be used to perform these vampiric talents, which I call Vampyrcraeft. Use of Vampyrcraeft drains excess essence quickly, and can even deplete the vampire's raw life-force. That can result in the need to feed on more blood more often, or even, in extreme circumstances, the death of a vampire.

I do not usually practice Vampyrcraeft and, needless to say, I do not kill victims for the minor amount of blood I require to survive. I generally find female donors who are willing to part with a small portion of their blood and energy, in exchange for my company. I usually offer to make a small cut with my straight razor, which I keep very sterile, but more often than not, they prefer that I bite them, usually on the neck. This is more painful for them, but most of them seem to find it erotic.

My canines are only slightly more pronounced than those of an average person, and I have seen many humans with longer ones than mine. Mine have very small, sharp hooks on their tips which make penetrating the skin much easier. However, I by no means have what could be considered fangs. In my younger days I used to grow my nails long and sharpen them to points, but then I decided it really wasn't worth the effort.

I am naturally a nocturnal creature. My pupils are attuned to seeing in darkness and do not adjust well to bright light. My skin is also very fair and burns easily. I prefer to sleep during the daylight hours, as I am very sluggish and uncomfortable during this time. When forced to go out during the day, I cannot be without my sunglasses and leather trenchcoat, which provide some protection from the sun's rays. I am only truly alive during the night.

How or why I became a vampire is beyond my knowledge. I have theories, but only theories. I have met a few others of my kind, and although we became close quickly, after a short while we just seemed to lose touch. We are solitary creatures by nature. Our heightened sense of awareness, what could be mistaken for human paranoia, is one of our primary survival instincts. It does not allow us to have close relations that last for very long.

Obviously, I do not know how to "convert" others into vampires, or even if it is possible. Perhaps you must be born one. I don't know. Of all of the donors I have bitten, none have exhibited vampiric properties. I have never shared my blood with another, and that might very well be the method, though I doubt it.

When people hear the word "vampire," most often an image of the cinematic Dracula or other pop-culture vampires will form in their minds. Today it would probably be Lestat or Louis, who represent the most popular image. The cinematic and literary vampire has little to do with its slobbering forefather of folklore, and even less to do with the reality of vampirism. When you tell someone that you are a vampire, they disbelieve because you do not fit their conception of what a vampire should be. I met a young girl at a restaurant once who asked if I was in a band. I jokingly said "No, I'm a vampire." She replied, with some authority, that I couldn't possibly be one because the smell of food would make me gag. Her personal conception was that a vampire could only drink blood, could not consume ordinary food, and that the very smell would sicken one.

The vampires of folklore were said to be walking corpses, damned to remain on the earth for committing some great sin, such as murder, suicide, or possibly, just being different. They were said to be denied eternal rest by God, and were forced to walk the night and drink the blood of the living to maintain their unholy existence. When vampire attacks were reported, the villagers would exhume the suspected corpse. After that, the attacks would usually stop.

I offer this theory to link folklore and true vampirism: The corpses of the dead, no matter how evil in life, were, by definition, dead. Still, people were attacked, weakened, and even killed. Disease may have been responsible in some of the cases, but often a shadowy form was seen lurking about the house of the victim, or fleeing into the night after the attack. And why did the attacks stop after the suspected undead was destroyed?

I submit that true vampires would watch a village until a likely candidate for mythic vampirism died. Maybe sometimes they would even secretly kill that person themselves, adding a mysterious death or possible suicide to the evidence of the victim's vampirism. Then, after the burial, the vampire would steal into homes, possibly *dressed in clothes similar to what the dead person was buried in, and feed upon the villagers. When the suspected corpse was then dug up and staked, the vampire would simply move on to a new place and to fresh blood. And thus the vampire attacks would cease. In that manner, a single vampire could simulate an epidemic of vampirism in a very large area, going from village to village, using his or her mythic cousin as a scapegoat, and thereby spreading the legend of the vampire.*

In closing I would like to say that I live and make no claims that I am undead. I show a reflection in a mirror or still water and do not deny it. I like a bit of garlic in my food once in a while, and am almost in every way like any other man or woman. But unlike others, I am a vampire. This I believe. Whether you do as well, is up to you. It doesn't make a bit of difference to me.

Dante's theory of how mortal blood drinkers could have been responsible for all the reported instances of vampirism in folklore is interesting, but really quite unlikely. That would mean that at some point in time, the mortal vampires of the world all decided to add to the legend that the dead can rise and feed off the living. Dante seems to feel that superstition led people to believe in vampires, and that mortal vampires were the ones responsible for any real evidence. What do you think? Does that theory account for the cases you read about earlier, or is it perhaps a bit too "thin" as an explanation?

One more thing before we move on: Dante mentioned meeting others of his kind. From the way he refers to them, it seems safe to assume that he felt they were a lot like him. Why don't any of the vampires in this book resemble each other closely? It's a question that makes it easy to believe they all have very different motivations for living as they do.

The Vampyr Virgo

This cryptic letter, although short, contains some interesting and original points. For starters, this vampire only casually mentions having been mortal before being "brought into" the vampire life; from that it seems we are to assume that she is claiming to be an immortal. That's interesting because most other letters seem to revolve around the vampire's mortal or immortal nature, while this one doesn't dwell on the issue at all. Is that because she accepts who she is and chooses not to "show off," or does she simply not feel like dwelling on a lie that is difficult to support?

What else is unique about this letter? Even though these two features can't be shown in book form, it is worth mentioning that this letter was written on parchment-like paper and was mailed complete with dried rose petals in an envelope. Perhaps that is not as important as the following question you might have asked upon reading the title of this section: What is a "Vampyr Virgo"? Read on and find out.

> *Well, I suppose sooner or later I would feel the insatiable need to tell my story. Actually, there is not much of a story to tell, but you may use what I write here in this letter in your book, if you wish. I know what I am—what I will always be for the rest of my existence. I am what is known as the Vampyr Virgo. Meaning, that when I was brought into this, I was a mortal virgin, which makes me a rather exceptional member of my race—and also very powerful. Powerful, because in this darkness reigns the glow of purity. Can you understand that?*
>
> *You asked in your ad of my lifestyle. I do not know that there actually is what is known as a vampyr lifestyle. It is not something chosen which is a "style." Rather, the way I live is something that is somewhat of an... instinct? Yes, that's it.*

Instinctively I am nocturnal. Sunlight hurts me. No, it does not really truly burn as legend has it. It only produces feelings of nausea. That is the closest human term I can recall to describe the feeling. Oh! And my eyes—they do water quite a bit in the presence of the sun. Also, they are extremely hypersensitive to all bright colors. I have a black-and-white television in my flat for that very reason.

And sadly... yes... I do need the (as I like to call it) "Elixir of Life" (blood) to survive. I say "sadly," because trying to acquire blood has become exceedingly difficult. I do have fangs as well as talons which I often get an inexplicable urge to tear at mattresses with. As you can imagine, I make quite a mess.

I will tell you one more thing: Do not fool yourselves, dear friends. You do not make a discovery here with me or any others of my species. We are as old as time itself. The books and films are simply what they are. Most do not even scrape the surface of the contents of our being. So do not try to understand. That would be like lifting eternal veils of a faceless bride.

There's really not much that can be said as a follow-up comment to that letter. One thing is for sure, however, if it's fiction, it's not a case of pure imitation. I included it here in part for that reason.

A True Immortal?

To finish this chapter, I thought I'd include one of the more "out there" letters sent to me from someone claiming to be an immortal. Although it sounds a little like popular fiction in places, the letter does include some points about the physiognomy of an undead vampire; you might find that interesting.

Also, if false, this letter makes a very good point about how seriously some people can take their belief in vampires. If someone could sit and write this vampiric letter as a fantasy, then it's easy to believe that same person would go out and act the part.

I have lived in death since April fourth, eighteen-hundred and seventy four, when a rather exquisitely beautiful woman named Monique invaded my mortal life. I fell hopelessly under her spell, or, should I say, became ensnared in her web as does the fly to the spider. She had long, erotic falls of midnight hair, eyes of the bluest summer skies, and a figure with all the right curves.

I tried, oh how I tried to defy her, to escape. But it was all to no avail. Then there came that penultimate evening; it was cold, so cold that the last of my mortal breath painted clouds on the Parisian air. She came as she always did, seemingly gliding on a cushion of sweet damp mist. I remember her smell. It was the only thing about her that disagreed with her alluring appearance. She smelt of the earth from which she had exhumed herself, of wet mud and autumnal leaves that rustled across the deserted roadways like sand drifts in a desert.

I closed my eyes and waited, longing for her. Longing for the pain of life to extinguish. Then when she reached me, I found myself waiting for the pain of her bite to fade. An intense pain it was; her long, vulpine incisors that gleamed so coldly in the semi-moonlight burst deep into my soft, warm, willing flesh.

Once she had found either an artery or a large vein, Monique began to suck the lifeblood from my body, the pain of the bite melting away in the heat of my arousal. It hurt, but I liked it, I wanted it to hurt. I needed it to hurt. I needed her.

She sucked and made a wet, dribbling noise, until the darkness roared in my ears. Until my mortal life ended.

When next I opened my eyes... I had changed. I gazed into a mirror, and saw the floral pattern of the paper on the wall behind me. My eyes saw as a feline's see. The night of my humanity had become light grey in immortality. There are no scents, however, for smell, like the other emotions of life and living, die along with the brain. My brain has well rotted in its case of bone. I move and survive by instinct alone.

My perception of mortals has changed vastly since my vampiric induction. I no longer consider you all as friends, enemies, brothers, sisters, or lovers. To me you are all prey. Simple, easy prey. I bare no grudges and hold no court over mercy or reprieve.

When darkness falls, I rise, kill, feed, and return to a place of safety before the blistering sun rinses my kind from the earth. Your blood has no taste or heat temperament, as these are messages passed through cords to the living brain.

It is in your mentality to label me as evil. To categorize me. Find a label you feel comfortable with, but there is no real label. You cannot categorize me.

I must take my leave. The eastern sky is a radiant blue—the hue of Monique's eyes—with tinges of a fiery orange at the very line where the land meets the sky.

You may have questions. With you and your kind there always are. For now, I hope you shall be content with the information I have given you here; feel free to use it in your book. I must go now. My stomach is full and the time for sleep is at hand. If I can leave you with one word, it is this: Believe.

[Signed D.P.E.]

That about covers our look at the letters of modern blood drinkers. It's beyond the scope of this book to include any more of those documents; however, we still have a few points concerning the vampires who wrote them to cover in the next chapter. As mentioned earlier, we have to address the dangers involved in blood drinking. That will be dealt with as part of the discussion on protecting oneself from mortal and immortal blood drinkers.

Chapter Six

Protection from Blood Drinkers

So far, we haven't concretely proven that immortal blood drinkers exist, right? Then why include this chapter? We haven't exactly proven that immortal vampires don't exist, either. But that's beside the point. The first part of this chapter will deal with the methods given in folklore for protecting against vampirism as well as destroying the offending creatures. Considering that very few, if any, who read these hints will ever come face to face with a true undead, the descriptions of the methods are kept brief and are mainly included to show what the past inhabitants of countries around the world believed. It is the possible occult significance of each belief that will make up the majority of each entry. After all, the possible esoteric truths behind the legends are what we are after.

Now that we've reiterated just how rare it is to run into a true undead, it's likely that some of you are relieved of fear, and probably quite a few are filled with disappointment. The next few lines are meant especially for those in the latter category. As the last chapter showed, some of those who would be upset at the thought of immortal blood drinkers not being real are the same individuals who might practice blood drinking themselves. If you've ever considered taking part in that dangerous practice, whether on the giving or receiving end, or both, please read the last section in this chapter carefully. Although the bits of folklore given in the next few pages might never come in handy, the factual information given in the last section could save your life.

Thwarting the Undead

Vampires are real.

Someone could have made that statement in almost any language, in any land, and at any time in recorded history, without being ridiculed. In any of those instances, there could have been many who personally disagreed, but it is likely that at least some did not. Those who felt the same way, and who came from the same land, likely also agreed on what the powers of the vampire are, and most important of all, how to thwart or even destroy the creature.

It is those shared beliefs that we shall now examine, starting with the more common ways to kill an immortal blood drinker, followed by a couple of methods for simply preventing such a creature from rising. Also included are some ways of keeping vampires that are running about from getting too close to either you or your house.

Keep in mind that a great many vampire countermeasures from folklore have achieved their own immortality in fiction. Let's begin our look at ways of killing the undead with a few of those.

The Wooden Stake

The wooden stake is without a doubt the most popular way in fiction to kill a vampire (not counting the power of the sun, the rising of which can't be controlled). In reality, it was, and still is, the most popular way to accomplish the task in Europe. Few people are ignorant to the fact that a sharpened stake should be driven through a vampire's heart to kill it. But what many don't know is why that should work.

First of all, let's look at a vampire as a human who is reanimated into a supernatural existence. How does the body of the creature function—when it ingests blood, is that blood circulated? In other words, does its undead heart beat? If that were so, then driving a stake through the organ and leaving it there would obviously disrupt the heart's ability to beat. Certainly, that might be one of the reasons staking was first implemented; we'll examine other evidence to support that theory in the related entry, "Heart Removal."

Another theory, put forth by vampirologist and author Raymond T. McNally, attempts to explain in a different way the beliefs of those individuals who performed the staking of vampires. According to McNally, the hunters felt that the power in this method came not from the stake itself, but from the earth. By driving the wood through a body, the bottom of its coffin, and into the earth, a hunter could effectively link an evil, animated corpse to the earth again, resulting in the vampire's decomposition.

A simpler version of that explanation, which many folklorists and vampirologists agree upon, is that the stake was meant to do nothing more than hold the vampire in place so it could not rise. Again, that depends upon the stake being driven clear through the body, the coffin, and into the earth. If the people of the past accepted that the stake only held a vampire in place and didn't actually kill it, that might be why the next method was often used in conjunction with it.

Beheading

While Hollywood special effects seem to be responsible for popularizing this method of vampire killing to life in modern times, it was used quite often in the past. Those who performed the decapitations of vampires were prompted by the idea that the act somehow ensured a vampire would not return from the grave. Why did they think that?

It is easy to imagine that vampire hunters of old knew that consciousness resided in the head. That is the part of the body, after all, where we process the majority of our sensory stimulation. Therefore, even if beheading a vampire didn't kill it (what vampire hunter could claim to fully understand the mysteries of the grave?), the creature wouldn't be able to hunt a human without being able to see, hear, or smell its prey. For that reason, the head of the undead was often simply placed by its feet, making it impossible for the vampire to pick it up again.

Clearly, even though the folklore of many countries contains tales of vampire beheadings, not all hunters felt the act ensured the true death of the creature. Besides placing the head of a vampire at its feet, another common practice was to place the decapitated head backward on the undead's neck so that even if it did rise again, it would not be able to see where it was going (they never seemed to consider the possibility that it might decide to walk backward).

If we consider our initial argument—that consciousness resides in the head—why would the hunters believe that the vampire might not die after it was decapitated? It seems likely that they believed removing a head from a supernatural creature wouldn't necessarily terminate the head's consciousness, any more than the physical cause of death in the person who became a vampire guaranteed he or she wouldn't come back. Decapitation was considered mostly to be a hindrance to a vampire. To be on the safe side, many hunters thought it wise to take a further precaution.

Burning

Vampires were often considered to be corpses animated by evil power. Burning the body of an undead therefore seemed to be a logical step to take. By separating and burying the remains, or by sometimes immersing them in running water and letting them be carried away, there would, of course, be no body left for the evil force to reanimate.

(A quick note before we move on: In many books, you will find the remains of vampire bodies burned on pyres referred to as "ashes." That is not accurate; the temperatures necessary to achieve the modern process of cremation could never be matched by a normal fire. However, we will not get into descriptions of the actual appearance of the resulting bone fragments and other unburned remains, which is too ghoulish a subject even for this book. Let's just say that the remains were not ashes, and could not be left for the winds to scatter.)

Besides the physical destruction that burning accomplishes, the process is thought by many to do much more. It is a common occult belief that burning something releases its mystical power, essence, or force. Certain plants and herbs are burned as incense to accomplish magical goals; candles are burned for the same reason. There are numerous other examples of rituals that use burning as a release of power, but it is beyond the scope of this book to go into them (if you are interested, see some of the books on magic and mysticism that are listed in the Bibliography). For our purposes, it is sufficient to state that burning the body of a vampire was probably considered a potent method of destroying the creature for more than one reason.

Heart Removal

This technique is not as widely used as the aforementioned methods, although it's sometimes used with them. Removing a vampire's heart represents a somewhat logical alternative to staking or beheading (depending on the beliefs of a particular culture). The heart keeps the living alive, and it pumps blood. Does it do the same for an undead? Cultures that remove the heart from their alleged undead might believe it does.

As we saw in Chapter Three, in the case of the vampire from the Greek town of Pyrgos, sometimes a culture's worst fears can be materialized. There, the *vrykolakas'* heart was seen to beat upon the opening of the creature's chest. Now, we know that the people of the area believed the heart must be removed to kill a vampire. So, is it possible that they saw what they expected to see, or were they simply correct in their belief?

By now you might have recognized that the basis for the practice of heart removal is similar to the idea put forth in the first "staking" theory given earlier. I mentioned there was further evidence to support the idea that vampires were staked to keep their hearts from animating them. The similarity of staking and heart removal cannot be denied, and it is possible that both practices could have stemmed from the same source. As with the other related bits of vampire lore covered earlier, similarity between two or more beliefs lends credibility to the vampire myth as a whole.

Holy or Blessed Weapons

A few obscure references to the use of some kind of blessed object against the undead can be found in folklore. In Eastern Europe, for example, a "sacred" bullet could be fired into the coffin of a vampire to kill it. It is not made clear, however, exactly how such a bullet would be made "sacred." Perhaps it would have to be blessed by a priest in the Orthodox Church (the predominant religion of Eastern Europe), or simply sprinkled with holy water.

On an occult level, the use of any blessed object against a supernatural creature could have a powerful effect. Practitioners of almost every type of mysticism agree that when an item is "charged" or blessed, it is infused with a form of willpower, as well as with an essence that becomes present on other levels. A good example of that is found in the practice of shamanism. Shamans can bring the spiritual essence or counterpart of an object of power along with them on their inner journeys, and can use it to work on other planes. Success in any such undertaking depends upon the shaman's belief in both the power of the item and in his or her ability to travel.

A similar principle would be at work if an item were blessed in ways that agree with a vampire hunter's religious beliefs. The hunter's belief in the religious potency of the object would make that object an extension of the hunter's will. Also, because the object would have a mystical essence of its own, it should be able to damage a supernatural creature in more than just physical ways. That is why exorcism rituals using objects such as a crucifix or holy water succeed; the occult essence of those objects would do the actual work on unseen levels. Of course, it can be argued that even if no evil spirits are present, the religious beliefs of the exorcist and the "possessed" person would make the ritual work.

Some fiction writers have picked up on the previous ideas, either through occult research or intuition. Many vampire stories and movies contain the idea that you must believe in a crucifix for it to actually work against an undead. Some fiction also presents the concept that the religious object used must be of the vampire's religion from when it was a mortal man or woman. If that were true, then it would agree with the last comment brought up about the exorcist and the "possessed" individual because the latter would have to believe in the symbols working for his or her benefit.

Next, let's look at a couple of ways to thwart an immortal blood drinker without "killing" it. These methods were used mostly to keep a vampire from rising from the grave in the first place. Some methods involve occult beliefs that are not exactly universal, but which were still common to many areas of Europe and the rest of the world. You might have noticed that the majority of the material in this chapter comes from European folklore. There is a motive behind that. The following chapters present the occult phenomena of psychic vampirism. The basis for that examination was partially derived from some of the commonly accepted principles of Western occultism, making the Western ideas presented in this chapter on blood drinkers relevant when covering psychic vampires.

Placing Holy Objects in the Coffin

In Europe, particularly in the Orthodox Christian countries, it is a common practice to bury the dead with either an icon, a crucifix, or both. This custom was originally intended to sanctify the corpse, making it impossible for an evil spirit to enter it. Keep in mind that the Church was not certain if vampires were possessed corpses or just corpses that somehow became animated by their own corrupt souls. If the latter was true, then the holy object buried with the body would act as a boundary that would keep the undead from leaving the coffin.

Placing Unsanctified Objects in the Coffin

In those areas of the world where Christianity was not dominant, and in a few where the religion did thrive, it was just as common a practice to put seemingly everyday, unsanctified objects in the grave as it was to place holy items there. Researching these practices is important because of the insight that they grant us to the types of superstition found in the world. More importantly, the customs are interesting because they show common beliefs about the afterlife.

Let's start with the location in the coffin where the majority of items were placed—near the head. Again, most cultures placed a great deal of importance on the head as the center of consciousness. That belief was so well accepted that, by association, the head and its orifices (the most important of which was the mouth) became known as the link to the soul—a gateway to the spirit world by which spirits could either enter or leave a body.

As for spirits entering a body, we've covered the idea that a vampire could be a corpse that is animated by an evil entity. So how could that be prevented? In Europe, bodies were often buried with items stuffed into their mouths. Those objects, which ranged from garlic to eggs, were thought to ward off evil spirits.

Although it's hard to distinguish between the two motives, sometimes the items placed in the mouth of a corpse were put there to keep the soul of the dead from escaping. That might seem a little bizarre at a glance to anyone who believes the soul moves on to some type of afterlife. However, that is not the process that was supposed to be halted; if a soul were to move on from its earthly remains, it would do so at the moment of death. If the soul had other intentions, like staying around to torment the living, then the objects placed in the corpse's mouth were meant to keep it from leaving the grave after interment.

Naturally, the last idea ties in with the belief that even blood-drinking vampires are not physical creatures, and that they rest only in their former bodies. This idea was popular because it seemed to account for how vampires could leave their graves without disturbing the soil, and how they could appear in any bedroom at night. (They would apparently materialize to attack.) As for how those spirit vampires would carry the blood back to the grave with them, little has been speculated. Regardless, the existence of the non-physical vampire was a widely accepted and feared possibility, and definitely accounted for a large number of bodies buried with wards against evil placed in their mouths.

As promised, we'll complete this section on thwarting the undead with a quick look at what was commonly done to keep immortal blood drinkers away after they had already risen. Who knows when these precautions could come in handy?

Sharp Objects

Like repels like in the world of folklore. Vampires have sharp nails and teeth, and therefore would be repelled by sharp objects like thorns and knives. The entrances to a house were the ideal spots to place such items.

Foul-Smelling Objects

Why was garlic supposed to repel a vampire? Once again, like repels like. Vampires were considered foul-smelling, and therefore would naturally hate garlic, as well as other substances with terrible odors, such as sulphur.

Objects of Mystical Power

The power of a holy item shows up numerous times in folklore. If vampires really are evil spirits (either ones that possess foreign bodies or inhabit their own), then an object of power might prove effective as a ward. However, you can't always be sure how potent the ritual that charged the object was (more on that in Chapter Ten).

Distractions

As odd as it might sound, people have put nets in their windows or sprinkled seeds around their property to keep vampires from entering by distracting them. Those who performed these countermeasures believed that a vampire could not pass a net without untying each knot. The seeds served a similar purpose—a vampire would have to count each seed before passing. However, even if those methods worked (they don't quite fit in with any occult school of thought), they would only delay an inevitable attack.

Mirrors

The occult power of a mirror is recognized by many cultures; they are often used in magical rituals to reflect evil back to its source. It is commonly believed that vampires cast no reflection in mirrors (that idea most likely originated with the belief that a vampire is a solidified spirit, and has no real physical image to reflect). They could therefore be repelled by not seeing anything in a mirror. If vampires cast reflections, then they might just as easily be turned away by what they do see.

Mortal Blood Drinkers: Dangerous?

The true undead is not the only type of blood drinker to fear. If you read the letters in the last chapter, then you already know something of the other type. They might not seem deadly—that's because, for the most part, they don't mean to be. The mortal blood drinkers who wrote the letters in Chapter Five seem considerate enough to drink only from willing donors. Chances are they aren't violent people who would kill those from whom they drink, intentionally at least.

If you would ever consider letting another person drink your blood, or have thought of drinking from someone else, consider this: There might be something just as life-altering in the blood of a mortal as in the blood of an immortal. That something is AIDS.

Scientists still have not isolated all the ways the deadly disease can spread, but they are certain that it is in an afflicted person's blood. Exchanging blood with someone with AIDS would ensure that you would get it as well.

What can a mortal vampire or donor do to protect him or herself? If the vampire or donor does not have AIDS, and is in a monogamous relationship with another vampire or donor who does not have AIDS, then the risk of AIDS is eliminated. However, AIDS is not the only thing to worry about.

The human mouth is not exactly germ-free; bacteria are present. Allowing such bacteria access to another person's bloodstream is not a very good idea. To make the explanation simple, antibodies and certain organs in the body clean blood of impurities, but those impurities can still make us ill.

Also, just how safe is the wound made in a donor? If it's too deep, and an artery or vein is severed, uncontrollable bleeding and maybe death could result. People have died of excessive bleeding during controlled surgery. Just how would a mortal vampire prevent such a terrible thing from happening when even medical professionals have failed in the past?

Furthermore, even if a wound made during a blood-drinking session is not deadly, is it sterile? Were sterile instruments used? Keep in mind that even if the wound is perfectly sterile, oral contact could cause an infection, for the reasons discussed earlier. Of course, for the same reasons, biting will almost certainly cause an infection, not to mention severe tissue damage, and possible excessive bleeding.

Finally, let's examine a minor danger inherent to the would-be vampire. Blood is a natural emetic. That is, a substance that could induce vomiting. Drink too much of it, and you could end up ruining that lovely cape. Of course, the amount of blood that induces vomiting varies in each individual, but it's another reason to avoid the practice of blood drinking.

In conclusion, to all the mortal blood drinkers reading this, I have this to say: Please reconsider your actions. Chances are, if you are reading this, you are interested in learning at least some of the mystical truths in our universe. Do not be in a rush to learn them all in the afterlife. The act of vampirism might sound glamorous to a fan of the creatures, but it really has no place among the living who wish to keep living.

We are finished with blood. Were this a typical vampire book, that would be a pretty ridiculous claim to make at this time (notice, there are lots of pages left). Next we're going to explore the types of vampires that occultists have proven do exist—psychic vampires—and they have no need for the red liquid.

Some who read the next few chapters might be startled by just how easy it is to be a victim of a psychic vampire. Don't worry; Chapter Ten will show you how to protect yourself from the creatures. And, unlike the methods given earlier in this chapter, the methods in Chapter Ten have been proven to work!

Chapter Seven

Psychic Vampirism

Remember the short scenario of supernatural attack at the beginning of this book? As the rest of this book will show, many people have experienced just such unpleasant, real-life moments of terror. Furthermore, statistical research has shown that the number of people who have had such experiences is significant. But what causes those horrible events?

It is possible that such nighttime attacks, referred to in at least one region as "Hag Attacks," are caused by psychic vampires, either unintentional or intentional. Of course, the night-terror description we're talking about is not the only way the creatures can attack. Psychic vampires can just as easily attack in full daylight, while the victim is wide awake, and even in public! As you can see, we've got a lot of ground to cover.

The Statistics

This section is rarely seen in an occult book. As most "debunkers" of the supernatural would claim, there is an apparent lack of statistical evidence to support the existence of the supernatural. That in turn provides great support to the arguments of "those who do not believe." But belief has nothing to do with reality.

Statistics are not included in most occult books because they are *not* collected, not because they *cannot* be collected. One just needs to know where to find the data. When dealing with psychic vampires, the best way to do that is to look for past victims without first letting on to them what their experiences really mean. In the following pages, we'll look at the results of just such a collection of data, which was undertaken in a completely scientific manner.

In Chapter Two, we briefly discussed the possibility of psychic vampire activity in Newfoundland, Canada. The people who live there believe that creatures known as "Old Hags" are responsible for terrifying experiences (similar to the one described in the beginning of this book) known as "Hag Attacks" or being "hagged." Folkloric explanations of exactly what Old Hags are supposed to be have varied over the years. For the most part, the Hags were thought to be witches or sorcerers who could astrally project to attack others (to clarify, the attacking "Hag" could be either male or female).

In the early 1970s, the Hag Attack caught the interest of David J. Hufford, a faculty member of the Folklore Department at the Memorial University of Newfoundland. His interest resulted in a research project that would occupy a good portion of the folklorist's time for the next decade. The enormous amount of information collected was published in Hufford's ground-breaking book *The Terror that Comes in the Night*, which carried the entirely accurate subtitle, *An Experience-Centered Study of Supernatural Assault Traditions.*

Apparently, Hufford was not the only student or teacher at Memorial University to research the Hag phenomenon. He managed to locate in the university's archives the results of a Hag survey and several documented accounts of Hag victims. With the help of those documents, Hufford was able to begin his own research with a basic knowledge of four events that, when occurring together, make up a Hag Attack.

First, the experience most often happens to someone upon awakening, and on occasion, right before going to sleep. Second, something is either heard or seen coming toward the room and, eventually, the bed of the victim. Third, the victim feels a weight on his or her chest that could seem as mild as a hand pressing down or as severe as a sense of being strangled. Fourth, the victim feels as if he or she is paralyzed and unable to make a sound.

When Hufford began to collect his own data on the phenomenon, he felt it would be best not to seek out Hag Attack victims but, instead, look for people who claimed to have experienced the symptoms of being hagged. There is a difference between the two. Were Hufford to ask immediately in a survey, "Did you ever experience the Old Hag?" then only people who had heard of the phenomenon could reply. Of those individuals, the chances would be good that their experiences (if any) were influenced by their knowledge.

To avoid that problem, and to make sure that all who had had the experience realized it had happened, Hufford worded his fourteen-question survey so that only the last two questions asked if the reader knew anything about the "Old Hag" or of anyone who had experienced it. No indication was given in the questionnaire that the "Old Hag" is the same thing as the experience defined by the individual's answers to the first dozen questions.

We won't be getting into the exact questions asked in Hufford's survey. If you would like to learn more about the survey, and would like to read some of the data collected by Hufford, I highly recommend that you read his book (see the Bibliography for more information). Because it was first published in 1982, it might be available only through used bookstores or perhaps your local library.

The questionnaire began with: "Have you ever awakened during the night to find yourself paralyzed, i.e., unable to move or cry out?" The questions that followed asked for other features of the experience, without giving any hints as to what Hufford knew was commonly experienced. Giving such hints would have been a bad idea, as the imagination of the surveyed individual might fill in any memory gaps with what he or she read on the page.

What were the results of the survey? We gave one result in particular at the end of Chapter Two. A surprising twenty-three percent of the people to whom Hufford gave his questionnaire had experienced at least the feeling of waking up paralyzed, one or more times in the past (those who reported having the experience several times claim that the attacks were usually spaced apart by months or even years). If that were all Hufford had learned, his statistics would hardly seem worth mentioning because it could be argued that waking up in a paralyzed state could be attributed to purely physiological factors (even though that seems highly unlikely).

The reasons Hufford's results were significant have already been suggested. Though the questions did not hint at the other possible traits of a Hag Attack, more than a few of those who replied that they had awakened in a paralyzed state gave further details about their experiences that agreed in many ways with those of their fellow survey takers. Many of the secondary features that were offered defined the four basic characteristics of the Hag experience mentioned earlier, while others added entirely new ones.

Now for more statistics. The questionnaire showed that roughly two-thirds of those who claimed to have awakened in a paralyzed state either knew about the Hag Attack or of someone who had experienced it. Though approximately forty percent of the people Hufford interviewed (students at the university) knew what a Hag Attack was, it's easy to imagine why those who had had the experience would know of it or of someone who had also suffered from it. Considering the fact that twenty-three percent of those surveyed had experienced the attack, it's likely that victims were often in contact with each other. Just bringing up the experience at a social gathering, for example, would probably bring out similar stories from other victims.

Some other traits of the Hag experience will be introduced in the following chapters when the cases of psychic vampirism I researched and witnessed are presented. A few of the incidents that occurred during the nighttime-attack cases resemble some of the experiences mentioned by the "hagged" individuals Hufford interviewed (the daytime-attack cases do not resemble the Hag experience, as can be expected). Keep in mind that none of the cases I became involved with took place in Newfoundland—that's significant evidence, as we shall see in a moment.

Before we go any further, I feel it is important to bring up a few key points. First of all, you might be wondering by now if the Hag Attack really has anything to do with psychic vampirism. At this point in the book, the connection might not seem entirely clear; however, I can assure you that it will be made evident. The Hag experience is a good starting point since the phenomenon was statistically proven to exist. Because it resembles apparent "supernatural attacks" that take place in other geographic areas, the phenomenon proves something strange is going on, possibly throughout the world. Is the cause of that "something strange" really a creature that thrives on the psychic energy of others?

Psychic Energy

If you hadn't known so already, then this book should have made it clear that a psychic vampire is not a blood drinker who knows what you're thinking or what the future holds in store. A psychic vampire is a creature, in either human or phantom-like form, that feeds on psychic energy. What do I mean by "psychic energy"? It's been known by many names in different cultures and time periods—Orgone Energy, Odic Force, Bioplasma, Chi, and Prana, to name a few. Whatever it's called, the energy is what seems to keep us alive and well; think of it as our lifeforce.

All living beings seem to generate at least some psychic energy; even simple plants have energy fields. The unlocking and application of that energy or essence is the basis of every psychic ability ever displayed, and is at the heart of every form of magic ever practiced. The information in the following pages is written in a way that assumes the reader accepts (for one reason or another) that psychic energy exists. For those of you who have never had a psychic experience (or never realized that you had one) or have never looked into the countless parapsychological experiments that conclusively displayed the effects of psychic energy, I hope you can at least read the rest of this chapter (and book, actually) with an open mind.

If all living things can generate their own psychic energy, why are there psychic vampires? Why would those creatures need to take energy from others? The answers to those questions further define types of psychic vampires. It's true that all living things can generate psychic energy, but dead ones that choose to remain bound to the earth can't. Also, some people, especially those who are old or ill, cannot generate enough psychic energy to survive. They unintentionally drain that energy from others.

Unlike the two types of blood drinkers, both types of psychic vampires can attack in the same ways, and to a victim, the attacks would most likely seem identical. The only thing that differentiates the way the two types of psychic vampires attack is their intention. Intentional psychic vampires know what they are doing, and willingly feed; the opposite is true for unintentional psychic vampires, as the term implies. One other reason I refer to intentional psychic vampires as such is because they not only willingly feed to survive when they are "dead," but also train themselves to do so while still alive in physical bodies.

Note: Just a quick word about how I gathered the information in the rest of this book. The "theories" presented in this chapter might be interpreted by some as just my "opinions" if I do not make the following clear: Part of what I say in these pages was discovered by comparing cases of psychic vampirism, and some was explained to me by the written teachings of intentional psychic vampires themselves. I've already said in Chapter One how intentional psychic vampires train themselves while still alive, usually with some kind of group guidance. By acquiring one such organization's teachings and comparing what is in those pages with the experiences of victims, I have been able to extract what I consider to be the occult truth from the propaganda.

The Occult Nature of Nighttime Attacks

The basic elements of this attack should be familiar by now. Sometime during the middle of the night, and on occasion at the time when one first goes to sleep, a sense of dread is felt. The victim of the experience finds it difficult to move, and notices that something is either already in the room or is approaching. Either way, within a few seconds of waking, the entity either becomes visible as a dark shape (sometimes with eyes), or is just "sensed" by the victim. At that time, the entity is seen or felt to approach the bed where it sometimes comes next to the victim or actually moves on top of him or her.

Once that "physical" proximity with the being is established, the victim usually begins to feel a weight pressing down on his or her chest. This weight is felt whether the vampire entity does and does not move on top of the victim, which implies that the pressure does not relate directly to the weight of the vampire, but to some other occult activity. (Quite possibly, the pressure is felt as a result of energy being drained from the heart chakra, but more on that later.)

As examples in the next two chapters will illustrate, the victim also notes other visual and audible sensations. The dark entity might take on some symbolic shape, or it might be surrounded by a colored light (I have encountered two examples of dark-purple light being reported by victims). As far as sounds go, victims occasionally report hearing voices or an echo-like, windy sound reminiscent of being in a tunnel.

The above sensations are the most common, but how can they be explained? Some would say the victims of such attacks are either dreaming or suffering from indigestion. I don't agree. What are the odds of numerous people dreaming the same type of waking dream, accompanied by similar sensations? Pretty slim; it's hard to imagine so many minds out there all enacting a psychodrama of nighttime attack. As for the idea of indigestion, I've heard of nightmares caused by eating something "heavy" like pizza before going to bed, but I can find no logical connection between suffering from indigestion and imagining that a dark assailant is in one's room.

Let's look at a future-science (occult) explanation of what is probably occurring during a nighttime attack. Most readers are familiar with at least the concept of astral travel, most commonly known as the "out-of-body experience" or "OOBE." Put simply, the idea is that everyone has an astral "double" or "body" that coexists with the physical body. With training, or sometimes by accident, one's consciousness can enter that body and leave the physical body, free to roam as a "spirit." At the time of death, it is also believed that the soul leaves using that astral body as a medium. (The astral body after death will be covered in great detail in Chapter Nine.)

For our purposes, we will say that the psychic vampire responsible for nighttime attacks is basically an astral body. Whether it is the astral body of a living or dead person, who is feeding intentionally or unintentionally, is unimportant for now. The differences between each type of "body" will be brought up with the appropriate supporting evidence later on. Again, for now, a psychic vampire that attacks at night is an astral body.

For some reason, in many cases possibly by pure chance, the astral psychic vampire chooses a particular victim. When that victim is chosen, the psychic vampire closes in. Depending on how psychically sensitive the victim is and how quickly the vampire moves, the victim will awaken to find the vampire either close to his or her bed, or approaching from a distance. I suspect the victim's psychic sensitivity is what is mostly responsible for the subtle differences between each case of nighttime-attack vampirism. Individual sensitivity determines when the victim psychically feels that something is "wrong" and awakens.

When the victim is awake, his or her psychic sensitivity establishes a number of other factors. First, it determines how much of the vampire is "seen" or "heard." If a psychic vampire is an astral body, then physical senses will not enable one to see or hear it. Astral senses, part of one's natural psychic sensitivity, are used instead. Some people are born with excellent faculties of that type, and others must develop them. (For more on astral senses, see some of the occult books in the Bibliography, including my own *Summoning Spirits,* which contains a chapter on the development of astral faculties.)

Another factor determined by the sensitivity of the victim is the level of "dread" that is felt upon awakening. It's interesting that those who see the vampire most clearly are the ones who feel the most terrified even before they see the creature. Apparently, it's not the sight of the creature that makes them feel terrified, although that adds to the feeling later. If we accept that those who see the vampire most clearly are the ones with the greatest sensitivity, then it seems likely that that sensitivity warns them of just how severe their "peril" is, and they feel a relative amount of dread as a result.

What about the paralysis? The explanation of why that happens is most likely one of the following: Either the victim's fear makes it impossible to move, kind of like the paralysis felt by someone who finds him or herself on a railroad track with a light approaching; or the vampire has some occult power over its prey (i.e., hypnosis), which could be a natural, unconscious, or effortless act on the part of the creature (remember, unintentional psychic vampires attack in this manner as well). Whichever force is responsible for the paralysis, it occurs in every attack and makes the victim an easy target.

Now for an examination of the actual feeding. For some reason, the vampire attacking in the manner we are examining needs to make astral contact; that means the vampire's astral body must touch the victim's astral body. The energy field of the body, or astral body, extends anywhere from a few inches to a few feet from the skin. For that reason, the vampire can simply float above the victim, or just "stand" next to him or her, and in either case still establish astral contact.

At this point in the attack, the actual energy transfer begins. The occult mechanism at work during such a transfer probably depends on whether the vampire is intentional or unintentional. In the case of some intentional vampires, they seem to learn how to take energy through an active mechanism (both during night and day attacks), but we'll explore that in Chapter Nine, where it can be described in the detail it deserves.

A simpler mechanism that can explain unintentional and, in some cases, intentional psychic vampirism, is osmosis. With the two astral bodies "connected," the energy would flow from the victim, who has an abundance of it, to the vampire, who has a depleted supply. When the energy level is equal between the vampire and the victim, it has taken all it can get, and breaks contact. That makes sense, because few victims of nighttime attacks report the experience lasting longer than a few minutes. Also, after they fall asleep again, the victims awaken feeling only a little tired, meaning that the amount of energy they lost had been for the most part regenerated by sleep.

Again, during the draining, pressure is often felt on the chest, regardless of the location of the vampire with respect to the victim. The pressure could be explained as simply an opposite force felt as a result of the osmosis process, or as mentioned earlier, could be a pressure generated by the heart chakra (one of the seven energy centers believed to exist in the body) as it loses energy. Why a vampire would take energy from that particular center is unclear. It is generally believed that a disruption of energy flow in the heart chakra causes anxiety. Maybe the anxiety caused by the experience has a reverse effect on that chakra and causes it to be more vulnerable to the vampire's attack.

When the attack is over and the vampire vanishes from the room (because it is in astral form, it is able to simply "fly" away through the ceiling or wall), the victim is somehow able to sleep again, probably helped along by the loss of energy he or she experienced. I mentioned earlier that the lost energy will be replaced in part by the time the victim wakes up in the morning. That is because the occult transfer of energy throughout the body seems to be easiest during sleep. The food we eat through the day possesses its own energy, and during the nighttime, we can fully absorb it.

Those who have read about magical or religious rituals will surely have encountered mention of fasting. Depriving oneself of food for several hours before any type of ritual, is done because the process of digestion draws away from the amount of available psychic energy. If you eat three meals, at seven in the morning, noon, and six in the evening, then your longest stretch without food while awake would be six hours. If you don't eat for a couple of hours before going to bed, and sleep for seven hours, you will go nine hours without food. Toward the end of that cycle, at about three to five in the morning, energy is free to distribute itself through your body.

Combine the fact that during the early hours of the morning digestion is not using up any energy, with the fact that the majority of individuals are asleep during that time, and it becomes clear why vampire attacks could easily occur then. Indeed, the hours of 3:00 to 5:00 A.M. are when the most nighttime attacks I have investigated have occurred.

Just a couple of last words on nighttime attacks before we turn to those of the day. If some vampires do feed using an osmosis-like process, then they will always be just a little less than "full," because they could never have more than what their depleted victims possess. Depending on how much of that energy they use from night to night, it is likely that psychic vampires might have to feed as often as every night. Considering the statements of victims who claim to have had the experience only once, or several times but separated by periods of months or years, it seems likely that each vampire feeds on many individuals—a scary thought! But, as you will see in Chapter Ten, there are ways to prevent that from happening to you.

The Occult Nature of Daytime Attacks

As is the case with nighttime attacks, daytime attacks can also be executed by either intentional or unintentional psychic vampires. However, I've never come across a daytime attack that can definitely be attributed to a dead psychic vampire. That probably has a lot to do with what I consider a daytime attack to be. What are referred to in this book as daytime attacks do not occur in astral form. The vampire attacking in this way has to have a physical body. Because dead psychic vampires exist only in an astral form (that, too, will be covered extensively in Chapter Nine), they cannot attack in the manner described hereafter.

There are rare cases of Hag-like attacks taking place in the daytime, but those are not covered here. That is because they occur only when the victim decides to take a nap in the daytime, and the daytime attacks we're introducing here happen when a victim is quite awake, and has been for some time. Daytime attacks can occur anywhere, and at anytime that can be considered part of the victim's "day" (it is possible that if someone works as a nighttime security guard, for example, he or she would experience "nighttime" attacks in broad daylight while sleeping, and vice versa).

We all know people who seem to drain all our energy when we are with them. Those individuals are often unintentional psychic vampires—people who for some reason (usually illness or old age) do not produce enough psychic energy to feel well. As a type of self-preservation mechanism, and partly due to osmosis, they act as a vacuum, "sucking" energy from those around them. The unconscious mechanism unintentional vampires use to accomplish that will be described in a moment, as it is similar to the conscious one used by intentional vampires.

You might be wondering why I claim that individuals who make others feel drained are often unintentional vampires.

From what I have learned about intentional psychic vampires, they try to vary their victims for the sake of maintaining secrecy. Therefore, if you notice that a certain person drains you of energy on a regular basis, then either the person is unconscious of his or her actions, or unconcerned about being discovered. It's hard to imagine the latter being true very often.

Let's move on now to the typical daytime-attack experience, and to the occult mechanisms at work during it. Unlike the almost melodramatic happenings of a nighttime astral attack, daytime psychic feedings are rarely noticed unless they are frequently repeated by the vampire. In most instances, the amount of energy taken, and the period of time in which it is taken, are both very small. A victim might, on occasion, experience mild fatigue if he or she is unfortunate enough to come into contact with a psychic vampire for too long a time, but that's the worst side effect usually experienced. No bizarre noises are heard, no phantom shapes are seen, and no pressure of any kind is felt.

Why the daytime-attack experience is relatively unimpressive is easy to see when the mechanism used by the vampire is analyzed. Whether the vampire is conscious of its actions or not, the feeding mechanism tends to develop through the following stages.

Touch

When a vampire first begins feeding, the only way for it to transfer energy is by bringing itself into physical contact with its victim. That ensures that the astral bodies or auras of both vampire and victim will provide a path through which energy can flow. If the vampire is unconscious of its actions, it will take some energy through osmosis whenever it comes into casual contact with its victim (through hugs, etc.); if the vampire is conscious of its actions, it will use a forced feeding mechanism.

Anyone who works with psychic energy for whatever reason (magic, yoga, etc.), knows that the flow of energy is linked to one's breath—inhalations bring energy in, exhalations expel it. In perfect agreement with that, the conscious vampire uses an inhalation to pull energy from a victim. Another accepted occult fact about energy flow is that it flows out of the body through the right hand in right-handed individuals, and out through the left hand in left-handed individuals. The other hand draws energy in, and most conscious vampires would probably use that hand for their feeding.

Close Proximity

After repeated feedings through touch, the astral body of a vampire becomes used to its ability to feed, and will start to form astral tendrils that seek out the astral bodies of others. Depending upon how long a vampire has been feeding on a regular basis, those tendrils could vary from a few inches to several feet in length.

Through astral tendrils, a psychic vampire could come into contact with whoever is nearby and still feed through osmosis, or if conscious of its actions, could mentally direct the tendrils to a particular target and feed through inhalation of breath. It is easy to imagine that a vampire that has been active for quite some time could create several such tendrils and feed off many individuals in a room at once. Next time you are at a social gathering, see if there aren't any individuals who could clear a room just by being in it for a while.

Eye Contact

Practitioners of tantric yoga and certain types of magic know that energy can be transferred by a gaze. Basically, the tendrils mentioned in the last level of feeding can be projected to greater distances if they are emanated by the eyes. A vampire that achieves the ability to do that can effectively feed from anyone who is in its line of sight. Depending on where you come into contact with a psychic vampire, that could make it rather difficult to avoid being drained (unless, of course, you use the techniques given in Chapter Ten). Unintentional vampires most likely never master this level; it seems too active a mechanism to be accomplished unconsciously.

Judging by how the cases of psychic vampirism I researched have progressed, and taking into account the type of self-training done by intentional psychic vampires, I believe the aforementioned levels of development to be accurate. Overall, the principle at work is that the aura or astral body of a psychic vampire develops to accommodate feeding. The astral body is flexible, and can be programmed to perform certain functions on its own. That will be the basis for some of the defenses against psychic vampirism given in Chapter Ten.

Chapter Eight

Unintentional Psychic Vampires

In contemporary fiction, vampires are often portrayed as tragic heroes who are unable to keep themselves from feeding. Their lust for blood overpowers their other desires and needs, and in many cases causes them to injure everyday mortals who befriend and try to help them. Fictitious blood-drinkers know their nature, yet they can do nothing about it.

What if a person is a vampire and doesn't know it? Wouldn't that make him or her the most tragic character of all? Imagine harming those around you and not even knowing that you are doing it, and on some level, not wanting to know that you are doing it; your vampirizing of others might be the only thing keeping you well or even alive.

These statements might not affect too many people who casually hear them. After all, how could fictional vampires not know what they are? It's pretty obvious that they would notice their fangs grow, and if not, they would surely notice when their fangs were buried in one of their victims' necks. But, as you know, we are not talking about that type of vampire anymore.

The type of vampire discussed in this chapter never notices when it is feeding, because there is nothing physical to notice. Its touch drains, its presence weakens those who are around it, and its unconscious nighttime visits terrorize—it is an unintentional psychic vampire.

Later in this chapter, we'll closely examine a case of unintentional psychic vampirism that I personally investigated. The events of that fascinating case are representative of the typical attack patterns that a victim of unintentional vampirism can experience. Most importantly, the incident also provides us with an insight to the unconscious motives driving the attacking vampire.

It's no exaggeration to say that the data gathered from that investigation helped bring together all my preliminary research on unintentional psychic vampires. As with the rest of this book, when we get to the case, I will let the facts speak for themselves. At this time I will say that the experience became the final test for the occult theories I had at that point only researched and developed and, as a result, nothing in the following pages is unverified speculation.

Let's establish a little more clearly what unintentional psychic vampires are and why they do what they do. We'll start with a basic definition.

Unintentional psychic vampires fit two important criteria: First, for a few possible reasons, they do not produce enough of their own lifeforce or psychic energy to feel well or, in some cases, survive. Second, they unconsciously develop and use the ability to take energy from others to gain the amount of lifeforce they need (or their bodies think they need). Those two criteria raise the following questions: Why and how? The answers are found in the two sections that follow.

Lifeforce

Each of the world's many mystical systems attempts to explain the mysteries of the universe. Of interest to us here is the fact that each system contains ideas as to what psychic energy is, how it is created, and how it works in the human body. We need to examine those concepts to discover why some people might lack adequate lifeforce of their own.

Rather than looking at countless theories on the subject of lifeforce in order to find out why some individuals might not be able to create their own supply of it, we'll instead combine some of the ideas that seem to "agree" when used together. Incidentally, that's how all occult theories should be looked at— as concepts that must still hold up when combined with other related theories. Just like all the laws and theories of thermodynamics work together, so too do those of the future science— the occult. Those who rigidly follow a particular school of occult thought might disagree with some of the liberties I am taking here, but I hope they can at least see why I did what I did.

So far, we have established that lifeforce or psychic energy is created by living things, no matter how simple or complex those creatures might be. Once created, that energy permeates not only the living being from which it emanates, but an area around the being as well. An inanimate object could become infused with energy through prolonged exposure to the aura surrounding a living thing, but inanimate objects can never create lifeforce. (By the way, psychometry, or the ability to psychically read the history of an inanimate object and those who have come into contact with it, is most likely made possible by the psychic energy that "rubs off" on inanimate objects.)

For our purposes, we will accept that energy exists in a field both within and around living things. But the form in which it exists is not the form in which it is created. The life-force is actually generated in small quantities by each individual part of an organism. Although it's not clear at what level the simplest generation of energy occurs, let's consider for this explanation that the building blocks of life—cells—are where the most basic generation of lifeforce occurs.

It's easy to think of each cell in an organism as a biological machine, as each carries out its own function that supports life in some way. Just like the cells in our physical body burn calories and release energy that allows for the functioning of our life processes, the astral counterparts of those cells release trace amounts of static lifeforce. Every physical thing has its astral parallel, and the energy released during basic life processes also has an astral counterpart. I call the energy that is produced "static," because it does not have any particular motion or purpose—it just exists in a free-floating state.

Static psychic energy, like static electricity, can accumulate (anyone who has walked around a carpeted area and then touched a grounded object or another person knows that static electricity accumulates). The similarities between static fields of lifeforce and electricity end there, however. A field of static electricity is composed of a number of electrons, which surround some object (whether it is as large as a cloud or as small as a scrap of plastic wrap). As far as atomic distances are concerned, the field of electrons is not very "tight" because electrons repel each other. That is true with all like-charged objects in the physical world, and as a result, static electricity fields do not last long.

Unlike a field of static electricity, a field of psychic energy is more cohesive and lasts for a long time. Why? Because in the astral plane or level, similar "charges" or elements attract. Therefore, each trace amount of lifeforce generated by a cell in a body is instantly pulled into the field surrounding the entire body and is added to the whole. The more energy there is, the larger the field becomes, which is why it could extend several feet from the physical body, depending on the astral vitality of the person.

It might seem as if the only thing lifeforce does is float around and within a body. This is true to some extent, as it doesn't "do" anything on its own. Rather, the body takes from the lifeforce field what it needs. Again, cells release both physical and astral energy that is used to carry out life processes; the lifeforce field is a personal battery. Areas performing biological work need to draw from that battery, and as a result, more of the energy coalesces in certain parts of the body than in others, forming energy centers.

Certain energy centers, including those known as the chakras, are accepted almost universally. Some magical traditions might exclude some in their rituals or add others, but for the sake of familiarity, we'll stick with the basic, commonly accepted seven chakras.

Most electrical activity in the body occurs in the brain and spinal cord. The signals and impulses traveling up and down that bundle of nerves seem to polarize and make use of astral energy (for that reason, many popular psychic exercises practiced around the world consist, at least in part, of causing energy to move vertically through one's body). Lined up with the spinal column of energy are the seven energy centers, named for the areas of the body they are closest to. They are the Crown (at the top of the head), Third Eye (between, and an inch or so above, the eyes), Throat, Heart, Solar Plexus, Navel, and Root (at the base of the spine) centers.

When not enough energy flows through those centers, health problems can arise. The particular problems arising as a result of each blockage are not really what is important (see the Bibliography for titles of books about energy centers); for our purpose, it is sufficient to say that almost every type of illness could either be created by, or result from, a lack of energy flow to the centers. It is important to understand the reciprocal nature of energy blockages.

Two things happen if someone is suffering from a continual illness. First, energy blockages like the ones just discussed will occur, but that's not the worst of it. Also, every afflicted cell in the individual's body will not produce as much lifeforce as it would when in a healthy state. This means the ill person's field of available lifeforce will be relatively "smaller." When only a small amount of lifeforce is present to begin with, the negative effects of energy blockages are magnified (in other words, the little amount of energy present cannot fully circulate).

A similar condition arises in many elderly individuals. Although blockages are not necessarily present (unless the person has some illness), the decreased level of metabolic activity often results in a comparatively smaller amount of generated lifeforce. Fortunately, many older individuals tend to lead more relaxed lifestyles than they did when they were younger. That puts less stress on their lifeforce field, and results in many of them feeling "just fine." However, some elderly people have more of a drive to do things than their lifeforce can support. It is those individuals who might end up needing more energy than they can produce.

Having introduced these possible causes, it is important to note how frequently (or infrequently) they might cause people to become vampiric. For starters, I'll say this: Most unintentional psychic vampires are the way they are because of the first of the two causes—illness. And not just temporary illnesses either; many times the afflictions facing the vampire are of a life-threatening, or at least severely debilitating, nature.

Also, depending on the severity of the disease, the astral body of the unintentional vampire may seem aware of its dangerous condition and actively seek to help itself. The presence of that fight-for-life instinct results in the rapid power "advancement" of the vampires in which it is activated. As a result, vampires that have the most severe illnesses become the most dangerous and advanced (as the case presented later in this chapter will illustrate).

It likewise follows that active, elderly individuals make up the smallest number of unintentional psychic vampires. There is no self-preservation motive unconsciously driving their astral bodies to seek "nourishment." Rather, they unwillingly develop vampiric tendencies to maintain a certain sense of well being. Because elderly psychic vampires aren't feeding to keep themselves alive, they tend to develop weaker feeding powers than ill psychic vampires. From what I have seen, most elderly psychic vampires never get past the contact-feeding level of development.

The Unconscious Astral Body?

The existence of the self-preservation feeding instinct in ill psychic vampires, and the less serious, feel-well instinct in elderly psychic vampires, raises the question of just how much control we have over our astral bodies. Unintentional psychic vampires couldn't exist if the astral body didn't act on its own at least occasionally, right?

The fact that our astral bodies act of their own accord should not seem unusual. Our physical bodies have many functions they carry out all day, without our awareness of how they work. To make an adequate analogy, though, I won't bring up the obvious functions like breathing. Instead, because we are interested in what the astral body would do to keep itself going, we need only compare physical self-defense mechanisms.

What's most interesting about the unconscious actions an astral body can take is that it can do more than a physical body can. If you need to eat, the only thing your physical body can do is make you feel hungry. Then, if you still don't eat for quite some time, you will start to feel other side effects (maybe fatigue or possibly a headache). But you will never find yourself opening the refrigerator and fixing yourself a sandwich without consciously wishing to do so.

The astral body, when deprived of enough lifeforce for an extended period of time, can get itself "something to eat." Again, like attracts like when it comes to occult energies and forces, and when a deprived field of lifeforce contacts a stronger one, there will be a tendency for the weaker body to siphon some energy for itself. Over time, that ability will develop on its own, in the stages discussed in the last chapter. It's just a matter of conditioning or learning. Once the astral body absorbs energy, it finds it to be beneficial, and "learns" how to do it better each time, much as animals can be trained with the use of food as a reward.

Even though the physical body is more limited than the astral body in terms of obtaining sustenance for itself, the physical body does have mechanisms that activate when faced with the threat of starvation. Most would-be dieters are warned not to starve themselves because doing so actually makes it harder to lose weight. Nutritionists refer to this as a "starvation mode" the body puts itself into when it is not provided with enough food. Fat is not burned as readily, calories are used sparingly, and the only thing one ends up losing is muscle tissue. Of course, the body is not trying to get revenge on its owner's brain for deciding not to eat, it is simply conserving "fuel." What's most interesting is that it does so unconsciously.

So far, for the non-vampire (or most of those who read this), the self-preservation instinct of the astral body represents nothing but the potential for harm. It's not exactly good news to most to know that someone could suck energy from them without either vampire or victim knowing that it is occurring. Luckily, there is a way to have the astral body defend itself. In some, that ability manifests on its own, while in others it must be learned. As a result, successful feeding for a vampire depends on the prey. We'll use just one more analogy to illustrate this point, and the similarities between the physical and astral bodies in general.

The physical body has the unconscious ability to protect itself from the attack of foreign bodies (germs and bacteria). Everyone not suffering from some type of immune deficiency has such an immune system in his or her body; how strong it is depends on a number of factors, but it's there. When a germ invades the body, the antibodies of the human immune system attack the intruder and usually "dispose" of it. This defense mechanism, described in such simple terms, is surely nothing new to most who read this, yet no one is ever aware that it happens. Our bodies just "know" on their own when they must dispatch their disease-fighting forces.

Immunity to psychic attack is not an innate, active mechanism as is the physical immune system. In most individuals, the astral body's ability to protect against theft of lifeforce lies dormant. However, the good news is that it can be easily developed. We'll take a look at how to do that in Chapter Ten. Once the ability is activated, it will unconsciously work as a form of psychic immune system, providing constant protection from certain forms of attack.

A First-Hand Account of Unintentional Psychic Vampirism

With an understanding of the nature of lifeforce and the astral body, we can now examine the case of unintentional psychic vampirism that brought the theories in this chapter together. The facts and events of the case included here are complete and true, as I either personally witnessed, or was told by a first-hand witness, everything you are about to read. Because the case was so illustrative of the phenomenon discussed in this chapter, its description and the analysis that follows it will complete our look at this type of vampire. (As in Chapter Three, the true names of those involved in the following case will not be revealed. Initials will be used instead.)

Many scientific discoveries in history have been made by accident. This case, which provided me with extensive, verifiable data, is but another example. I learned of the vampiric incidents you are about to read through a peculiar sequence of events that I'll share briefly before we get to the heart of the case. Those circumstances are included mainly to illustrate just how common psychic vampirism is, and how it could affect either people you know, or you yourself (unless certain precautions are taken, of course).

One night in December 1993, a musician friend of mine—we were in a band together at the time—told me that he wouldn't be able to make it to practice because he had forgotten his mother's birthday party was that evening. He had promised her that he would go home after work (he still lived with his parents at the time). The others in the band were quite upset that he forgot to tell them he had made that promise, but I understood his predicament, having been in similar ones. I got on the phone with him, and he asked me to ask the others if they wanted to meet at his house so we could all be at the party with him, and maybe "save him from some boredom." I said I'd go to the party, but the rest of the band "didn't feel like it." I had no idea that my favor for a friend would have such a beneficial outcome.

When I arrived at the party, the house was nearly filled with guests. I didn't know anyone there, so as my friend got pulled here and there, time moved pretty slowly for me. I sat down near the front door, where there was an empty chair, and figured I'd wait a while to see how things went. A few minutes later, the door opened and a short woman with dark hair entered. She seemed to be in her fifties and wore a markedly sour expression. Several guests went over to her immediately, and one young lady took her by the arm to help her to the couch, but the newly arrived guest refused it. I assumed she must be a close friend or relative by the way she was received (and by the fact that she didn't ring the doorbell), but I couldn't figure out why someone had attempted to help the woman to a seat.

In a little while, B., my friend's mother, came into the area and noticed her new visitor. B. walked over to the woman, gave her a somewhat fake smile, and moved on. I could see that B. was upset by the guest's coming, although the guest herself did not seem to be uncomfortable being there. In a little while I learned who the guest was—we shall call her M.

To learn that the two were friends interested me because B. did not seem happy to see M. But that wasn't all that I found interesting about the whole affair. M. was apparently dying of cancer, and it was strange that her friend should seem cold toward her. Once I learned who M. was to B., and what she was suffering from, I couldn't imagine why her friend would give her the proverbial cold shoulder—I always felt that people should be there for sick friends.

After a while, I started to forget about the new guest. My fellow band member was once again free, and we were talking about the band's latest plans. After an hour or so, I started to feel tired and sat down. I had had a long day, and as I sat back, I felt myself enter a mild altered state of consciousness as a result of my slight fatigue. As I looked around the seemingly more crowded room, I noticed that M. had not moved from her seat. However, everyone had for some reason moved away from that part of the room.

I found that odd, and in my relaxed state of mild boredom, I let my gaze fall on her. What I saw positively shocked me, mostly because it was so unexpected. The lady looked like some kind of human spider! I knew that what I was seeing was not physical, but an astral vision as a result of my altered state. After the initial shock wore off, and I checked to see that no one was staring at me, I let my gaze fix on her once more. Again I saw the awful sight.

She was surrounded by a dark purple aura that emanated about two feet from her body. Toward its edges, the aura seemed to darken so that it looked almost black, yet the darkened area did not prevent me from seeing through it to the purple area. From the dark edge of the aura, several thin, black tentacles were protruding and moving toward the group of party guests. I watched for no more than fifteen or twenty seconds, when M. turned and looked at me. Not sure of what to do, I just smiled at her. She returned my smile. As I watched the tentacles continue their swarming, I realized she had no idea of what she was doing at the moment. I must have looked confused, for I heard my friend call over to me, asking what was wrong.

I immediately went over to him, and tried to act as if nothing were wrong. The whole time, however, I was trying to decide if I should say anything to him. It was no secret to my friend, or to the others in the band, that I was involved in occult research and experimentation. At the time, I was putting the finishing touches on my first book and had invited my friends to a few lectures I gave on magic at a local university. Even though he knew of and respected my occult interests, I wasn't sure how to explain to him what I felt I knew—that his family friend was a psychic vampire!

While I was still trying to decide what to do, B. came over to ask me how my girlfriend was doing. I took advantage of her question and got into a conversation with her. After a while, I casually brought up the fact that I didn't feel very comfortable over by the couch for some reason. She immediately froze and looked at me almost searchingly. Her son had told her of some of my interests and I wasn't surprised when she asked if I would "help her get something from downstairs."

When we got to the basement, B. told me that the very night before the party she had what she thought to be a horrible waking nightmare. In the early morning hours (she wasn't sure when, just that it was still dark), B. awakened to find that she couldn't move (as you might have guessed). According to B., her head felt as if it were "swelling and thundering from some kind of weird vibration," and her chest felt as if someone were "pushing down on the covers."

She went on to say that she remained still for a few seconds, sweating and terrified. Then, she suddenly became aware of a sound resembling hollow wind. Hoping it was her husband waking up, she tried to call out to him, but no sound came from her mouth, and her husband wasn't stirring. In a few seconds, the windy sound grew louder and she began to notice a purple light swirling over her.

I was extremely interested at this mention of purple color, as I felt what I had noticed upstairs might somehow be connected to the experience B. was relating to me. I remained quiet, though, to let her continue.

The purple light formed into a shape that B. recognized immediately. It was a serpent, with its coil resting on her chest. Her terror was so great at that moment, she told me, that she could hear her heart beat and could feel pain from the scream that couldn't escape. The pressure on her chest grew for a moment and the serpent opened its mouth. As soon as it did so, its head vanished and was replaced by a black sphere. In it, B. saw M.'s face clearly. There was no expression on the phantom face and its eyes were closed.

In another few seconds, the entire vision vanished, taking with it the pressure and sound that B. experienced. The feeling of immediate terror passed as well, but B. said she still felt scared when thinking of it. Seeing M. at the party brought back her fear, and for some reason, she couldn't dismiss what "must have been a dream" and spend time with the dying woman as she usually did. Something "didn't feel right" about M. at the party, "or lately, for that matter."

At that point, I shared some of my theories on psychic vampirism with her, and explained what I believed yet had never proven to myself (until that night, that is). I won't get into the details of our conversation that followed. B. was scared by what she learned, but was at least happy to learn that M. most likely had no idea of her vampiric preying, and if she did, was definitely not doing it on purpose.

We talked for a while, and I promised B. that after most of the guests left, we would talk more. B. tried to seem more friendly to M., and I could tell the ill woman was pleased with the effort. After the party, as promised, B. and I talked more. My friend and his father were busy watching a movie and didn't pay any attention to our conversation, so I felt free to tell her what I proposed she do that night.

B. confessed to never having practiced even the simplest meditation before, and was a bit hesitant about the techniques I explained to her. They seemed like magic to her, and she wasn't sure she could carry them out. I told her they were magic, meaning it would be her will that would be carried out as a result of her performance of the techniques.

In Chapter Ten of this book are instructions and preventative measures the reader can take for protection from psychic vampires. The basic forms of those rituals or techniques are what I told B. to attempt on her own that night, after some assurance that there was nothing evil about protecting herself with "magic," and that she could make the rituals work. B. promised she would try, and soon after I left the house.

The next day I called B. and asked her how she slept. She said she had slept soundly and thanked me for the magical techniques. I explained to B. that she should reinforce her protective measures from time to time because M. might not have come to visit her that night anyway (I knew that Hag victims were rarely attacked two nights in a row), and M. might come back soon. Sure enough, eight days passed and the vampire did return.

B. told me that she woke on the eighth night and felt a presence in the room; however, she didn't feel any terror, or the pressure in her head or on her chest. She thought she heard a bizarre "electrical" sound coming from the corner of her room. Finding she could move, she sat up and looked in that direction. She saw a faint purple light, this time broken up in tiny floating sparks; the image lasted a couple of seconds and faded away. The sound ceased then, too. That was the last time she was ever bothered at night by a phantom visitor of any kind.

As for M., she moved out of state to be with some relatives. She apparently went into remission for a while, though I'm not sure of her current condition, as B. hasn't been in touch with her for quite some time. It's unfortunate that M. moved, because I would have liked a chance to help or at least talk with her, although I'm not sure exactly what could be done for her. Most likely, she went on to prey on other victims.

In this chapter, and in the previous one, I introduced most of the features of the attacks just described: the formation of astral tendrils or tentacles, the sounds heard during a nighttime attack, and the presence of some color or shape. The swelling feeling that B. experienced in her head is not commonly reported in attacks of this type, but is one example of the minor variations attack victims experience.

I would like to say a couple of things about both the color and shape B. saw at night. In this case, a good argument can be made for why the apparition in B.'s room was purple. As my own experience showed, M.'s aura or energy field was purple, making it easy to accept that purple would be the color psychically seen by someone if M.'s astral body entered the room. But understanding why the vampire took on a serpent form is more difficult.

One interpretation can be arrived at by examining B.'s religious beliefs. As a practicing Christian, her personal cosmology includes the existence of the devil, the serpent of the Old Testament. Perhaps the impending spiritual danger translated itself to a symbolic form that she would understand as something dangerous to her psyche.

That just about does it for our look at unintentional psychic vampire attacks. Because those vampires are always living people, we had no need to delve into examinations of the "dreaded hereafter." The nature of the intentional psychic vampires described in the next chapter will require us to examine the concept of spiritual immortality—including its various forms and the "price" of each.

Chapter Nine

Intentional Psychic Vampires

These are the darkest creatures. Although they start out as humans, upon their mortal deaths, intentional psychic vampires can become monsters in every sense of the word. Like vampires of fiction, intentional psychic vampires also go through a transformation that grants them eternal "life." However, that immortality is not experienced in a material form. Also, while the undead of fiction are often created against their will, the psychic vampires dealt with here freely choose to become what they are.

How do such vampires transform themselves, and why do they do it? What could possibly be the benefit of existing forever among the physical inhabitants of the earth as a non-physical spirit vampire?

Apparently, intentional psychic vampires feel there is great personal power in being able to survive on the energy of others. Some of those people even congregate on occasion, which is why there are organized groups of people with the goal of the perfection of psychic vampirism. Some individuals who practice vampirizing others are aware of the transformation they could someday undergo; in fact, the change into an astral vampire motivates many of them.

Other psychic vampires practice only with thoughts of the here and now. They just want to be able to make others weak and themselves stronger while they are alive. They often don't think about the afterlife, and don't consider what will happen to their developing astral bodies after death. However, the fact that they do not plan on being around after their hearts cease beating does not mean they will stop being psychic vampires when they die.

The following discussion will touch upon topics that almost every religious person in the world has strong feelings about. However, my purpose in presenting this section is not to present or disagree with any religious beliefs. We will be looking at life after death from a purely occult-science approach, acknowledging that there is something after mortal death. Although it might be a glorious state of being that we are all destined for, we will not speculate as to what that existence might be like, or what deities might be present there. Like many occult theories, what you are about to read has been drawn together from many sources. In this case, some of the work of occultist Dion Fortune played a role of chief importance (see the Bibliography).

As in other sections of this book, what you are about to read cannot be completely proven. However, when the occult ideas presented in the following section (and in the rest of the book) are studied in light of the facts of the case described later in these pages, they do appear to be accurate.

The Second Death

Many occultists of both yesterday and today accept that within the physical body there are at least two other subtle bodies:

the astral body, which we can consciously enter and travel in; and the mental body or soul, which is our true consciousness or being. Those subtle vessels do not die with the physical body, as they are not maintained by only physical means.

When a person dies, his or her astral body is released, containing within it the soul. The separation of those bodies from the physical shell is complete at that time, which means that when they leave, they take with them all the psychic energy surrounding the now-lifeless physical body. After all, that energy was being used by the astral body only, and it naturally leaves the corpse using the vessel it "powers."

The newly freed subtle bodies can exist in this free-floating form for an amount of time determined by one factor only—how long the psychic-energy field surrounding the astral body can remain intact to keep the form alive. Without the matching chemical processes of life causing the astral body to generate new lifeforce (as discussed in the last chapter), the astral body will eventually use up its surrounding field of energy as it tries to keep itself going (many occultists believe this might happen as soon as twenty-four hours after physical death). Once the field of lifeforce is consumed, the astral body will experience what is known as the "Second Death."

When the Second Death occurs, the astral body dissipates and the soul or mental body that was animating it is free to move on to the afterlife. Depending on what type of life the soul led, it might not always be eager to see what lies ahead. This is another example of like attracting like. If a person does evil deeds in his or her life, such as vampirizing the lifeforce of others, then he or she will most likely attract evil energy or be attracted to a region of it. In other words, an evil soul would probably sense a dark future awaiting it.

Assume that before the Second Death, the soul, still within its astral body, somehow "feels" a weakness coming on. Whether it is motivated by a fear of what the afterlife might hold, or simply by a fear of "dying" again, the soul might decide to keep its astral body alive. An intentional psychic vampire who has been training for eternal life as a spirit would probably know how to keep its astral body alive, but a person who actively practiced being a vampire might come to realize what can be done only at the moment of Second Death. Therefore, in either case, it is possible that the soul will decide to "feed" its astral body, keeping it alive and earthbound. After all, the earth is familiar, and the soul would feel most comfortable here, safe from the unknown darkness.

How such a vampire could keep its astral body alive is simple. If it has ever fed off someone in astral form when alive, it already knows the procedure (I am referring to the nighttime attacks we already discussed). The astral body of the deceased would simply have to visit its victim at night, steal some energy, and leave. But "where" would the astral body go when it's finished with its night of feeding?

It seems likely that, because of the sympathetic link a soul would feel with its former host body, the astral body would be naturally drawn to spend the non-feeding hours (in most cases, daytime) in its corpse. If that were the case, then the residual lifeforce surrounding the astral form might cause the physical body to remain somewhat preserved, which could explain several cases of vampirism in folklore. Perhaps, like B. in the last chapter, the victims of such psychic vampires saw their assailants' faces and caused their corpses to be dug up. As we'll see later, psychic vampires could cause "bite" marks to appear on their victims, so it's likely that people could mistake such an attack for one that draws blood. After all, our ancestors had no way of knowing if a victim of vampirism who looked weak had actually lost blood, not just psychic energy.

It seems that a vampire might be able to carry on feeding in that manner forever. Considering what we know about the eternal nature of energy, there's no reason the energy-feeding process should one day stop working. As long as a vampire's astral body absorbs lifeforce it should remain intact, and most likely, could grow more tangible. Manifestations of apparitions could be little more than glimpses of such earthbound vampire spirits.

Though the soul in its astral form is escaping the unknown hereafter, what kind of "immortality" is it experiencing? There are plenty of horror and science fiction stories dealing with a person who can't interact with others—someone who for some reason is invisible, and can only watch others enjoy life. That could cause anyone to go insane, possibly even an intelligence that no longer has a physical mind. Could such angry vampires, who were made strong through years of astral existence and feeding, be responsible for the vampire "plagues" of years ago? Probably not, because there is no reason such outbreaks wouldn't happen today, too. But the possibility of a psychic vampire deprived of physical life becoming extremely violent because of its condition does not seem all that remote (we'll look at an example of a violent psychic vampire later in this chapter).

What about the victims? What if a psychic vampire were to take a life? In folklore, it was often believed that whoever was killed by a blood-drinking vampire would eventually rise as one. Could the same hold true for those who die of energy loss?

First of all, let me make it clear that I know of no cases in which it can be proven that a person was killed by a psychic vampire. In other words, I've never found a case where a person was a frequent victim of vampirism and died as a result (if a person was attacked only once and died, how could we ever know?). However, that doesn't mean it never happened. The search for an authentic case of that type is difficult because even if a death was caused by psychic vampirism, it would most likely appear to have occurred as a result of natural causes.

The theory that victims of psychic vampirism could become psychic vampires themselves has been "floating around" for years. Proponents of the theory include Dion Fortune, who had much to say about psychic vampires and attacks, but to accept the theory as it is seems to be unwise. When compared to some of the other theories discussed in this book, the idea just doesn't hold up. If the other theories we looked at earlier are accepted (they do seem to be correct when they are applied to cases of psychic vampirism), then whether a victim of a psychic vampire also becomes a vampire most likely depends on the cause of physical death.

If a person who is frequently attacked does not die of energy loss but by some accidental fashion, then he or she should be in a more-or-less healthy astral condition. Just as we discussed earlier, the physical body of a victim can regenerate most of the energy that is lost, often at a rate that results in the victim not even noticing that anything more than a bad dream was experienced. Should the victim die while in such a state, it seems likely that the natural process of astral death and release would follow. There is no reason the astral body would "hunt" for vitality. Because of the quick regeneration of lifeforce in an otherwise healthy victim, the death of such a person could be viewed as the death of a person who had a normal amount of lifeforce within his or her body.

Some occultists do not agree with that idea, though, and have put forth the idea that victims would become psychic vampires even before death. The reasoning behind this idea is that someone who is drained by a psychic vampire will become a psychic "sponge." Why this should happen cannot be explained, because a healthy person could easily regenerate lost lifeforce. It would be more difficult for an astral body to try taking energy from someone else. We saw earlier in the book how astral bodies progress in their levels of feeding development. It's unnatural and difficult for a weakened astral body to seek out its sustenance "elsewhere," but hardly any effort at all for a healthy body to simply generate its own psychic energy.

What about those who die of energy loss? When that occurs, everything changes. In such cases it seems likely that the theory of victim-turning-vampire could hold up. Why? Because if a person dies as a result of having almost no energy in his or her body, then the only way energy could be acquired is through vampirism—the dead body could no longer produce it. Think of the astral body of a person who died of energy loss as being in a state of shock. In many cases, the released astral body could simply dissipate as in a normal death (although this decay would be somewhat accelerated). In some instances, it could seek to recover from its weakened condition.

An astral body of someone who is dead does not have to learn how to move about freely to hunt for sustenance. It seems likely that in the moments after death the astral form could be drawn "magnetically" to a source of the energy it needs. A sleeping person in the vicinity would be a perfect target, and if the original victim dies during a nighttime attack, most people in the area might also be asleep. That means the free astral body would have little difficulty finding a relatively helpless victim.

It is unclear if the astral body can instinctively feed. Perhaps the same self-defense mechanism that makes an ill individual feed off others would be at work, but at a stronger level. After all, the astral body would be at the point of Second Death immediately after physical death. There would be no natural dissipation of the astral body, but an instant energy deficit that the phantom form might feel the need to correct. If the astral body were to become used to feeding off others, it's likely that it would remain a psychic vampire, grow in strength, and consciously seek to maintain its dark existence. Therefore, even though such a vampire would be considered unintentionally created, the consciousness of its nature it would develop over time makes it, for our purposes, an intentional psychic vampire.

Intentional Psychic Vampires ☞ 159

As you can see, psychic vampires could be around for a long time because their activity is not dependent upon the survival of their flesh. The moment of physical death for an intentional psychic vampire, or of someone with the potential to become one, is only the beginning of the creature's most active stage of vampirism. If the theories about the Second Death and avoiding it, are correct, that stage can last for a long time.

To show what intentional psychic vampires might be capable of, we'll now look at a case of vampirism that, if true, can be safely attributed to this type of creature. Through the analysis of the facts in this case, we should be able to identify more easily the subtle traits of the vampires. The vampires presented in the pages that follow seem to have succeeded in escaping their Second Deaths. They might still be out there....

The House of the Vampire

This incident occurred in the spring of 1994, only a few months after my success at helping B. with her case of vampiric attack. As was the case with that incident, I wasn't actively looking for a report of vampirism. However, the surroundings where I first heard of this case were more conducive to this sort of discussion.

I was attending a psychic fair in my area and, throughout the course of the evening, had conversations with several people about the "unseen world." Many of the conversations had to do with the book I was working on at the time (*Summoning*

Spirits). After a few hours, when I found myself alone, a man who looked to be in his late twenties or early thirties approached me and introduced himself. We shall call him S.

As I learned from him, he had been listening to me talk about the nature of entities and was waiting for a chance to have a word with me in private. He claimed to have a serious problem, and wanted to know if I could help him. I told him I would listen to what he had to say, and sincerely expressed my interest. He looked like he was honestly troubled, and I was curious to see why my conversations about the nature of entities would make him think of his problem.

After we agreed to move to the outside hall of the building, S. began his tale. He said that for the past three months or so, he had been living on his own in a new house. After just a few days there, he began to get the impression that something was "wrong" with the place. He said that he wouldn't exactly have called the house "haunted" at that time, but rather, "charged." No matter what he did, he couldn't shake the feeling that the house was not a good place to be. The hairs on his body would often stand on end when he entered certain rooms, and he would sometimes feel like he was walking through cobwebs, though he could see none.

At first he attributed the tingling sensations he felt to his imagination. The house, which he got for "a great price," had been abandoned for several years, and he thought that all the horror movies he had seen over the years were catching up to him. He didn't hear any voices or see any phantoms, so he tried to ignore his impressions for the first few weeks.

Then he started noticing that he was beginning to feel tired a bit too often when at home. However, he couldn't logically come to any conclusions as to why, in addition to feeling the occasional strange sensations, he wanted to rest constantly. Thinking something was wrong with him, he went to his doctor, who could find nothing physically wrong. The doctor suggested that perhaps S. was working too hard, but S. told me that right before moving into his present home, he was promoted to a position where he was more of a supervisor than a doer. That meant that he had fewer job-related worries in his life than he ever had before.

I didn't want to offer any suggestions yet, but I had a feeling as to where this was going. Like I said, it had been only a few months since I helped B., and the events of that case, and the impressions I received from it, were still fresh in my mind. I didn't want that tale to influence S.'s story, so I kept quiet. I thought that he was somehow the victim of daytime psychic-vampire attacks, and considering what he told me next, he most likely was.

My suspicions were confirmed when S. told me of an experience he was having regularly—about twice a week, but never two nights in a row—in what he called the early morning hours (not surprisingly, he said it was often just before five o'clock). On those occasions, he would awaken in a state of absolute fear, and find himself unable to move. (That should sound familiar by now.)

After being awake for a few moments, S. would notice that he wasn't alone. Several dark forms—he estimates around six or seven of them—would surround his bed. He said he couldn't make out any features on the spectral intruders, but could see only that they possessed anthropomorphic forms (i.e., their general outlines looked humanoid). For what would seem like hours, although probably only a few minutes, S. would remain in bed, paralyzed and afraid, while the figures stood quietly in their positions.

Then, after the seemingly long wait, the level of S.'s fear would increase with what occurred next. Looking to the window in his room, he would notice a dark purple light appearing in it. The glow would spread into the room for what seemed like a few feet and form a semi-sphere, with the flat part of it positioned against the window and its "hump" coming into the room.

At that time, S. would hear sounds coming from the area of the window. He told me it sounded like his window had been opened, but not to the night outside. He said the "echoes and rushing sounds" coming from that part of the room often made him scared to think of where they could be coming from—they couldn't have been coming from anywhere "nearby." Again, I didn't want to put suggestions into his head and taint his story, so I did not comment on his obvious suspicions that some kind of wall between worlds was being breached.

Finally, after all the waiting, the experience would near its climax. S. would notice a larger, yet still vaguely humanoid, figure appear in the purple light. The larger one would move, slowly making its way toward the bed. After another seemingly endless period of waiting, the figure would reach the bed and the others would move a little closer, as if trying to get a better look. The large figure would hover over S. and its form would stretch to the point where it resembled a giant blanket of darkness. At that time, S. would notice its red eyes.

Even though the phantom seemed to be at least two feet away from S. when it was closest, S. would begin to feel "a very heavy weight crushing his chest" while the figure was hovering above him. Accompanying that sensation was the sense that the sounds he had originally heard coming from the window had entered his head. S. claimed that the roaring in his head, combined with the pressure on his chest, made him feel like screaming in agony, but he couldn't. He could do nothing more than just lie in mute and paralyzed terror.

The pressure would build and the sounds would get louder until both reached levels that S. thought were the limits of his body's endurance. Then, both would increase in intensity even more, and S. would be on the verge of losing consciousness when he'd notice all the figures getting closer. He would then black out and awaken later, sometimes after sunrise, to find his room empty and the sensations gone. However, he would feel very weak, and on some of the days when he had to go to work after such an experience, would call in sick or use one of his vacation days.

That's where S.'s first tale ends, but not his entire story. When he finished speaking, I tried to explain to him what type of being was most likely bothering him. I didn't want to alarm him, but his story contained severe, uncommon elements, which were most likely very dangerous for him. For one, I was shocked to hear of how often he was being attacked, and by how many vampiric entities. What really made me worry about his well-being was the apparent intensity of the attacks. I had never read or heard a case in which the victim would black out and be unable to function the next day. To say I felt sorry for him is an understatement—imagine having to endure that type of experience twice a week!

The whole time S. was telling me about his experiences, I could see genuine distress in his features and his movements. I hadn't spoken to anyone about psychic vampires at the fair that night, so I knew that S. had no obvious reason to play a joke on me, and because I had the general impression that he was telling the truth, I decided to take his phone number and make plans to further investigate his case. Not only was the information I was gathering of direct relevance to my current research, but as I said, I really felt badly about his situation and wanted to try to help him out.

Before we parted company at the psychic fair, I decided to do more than just explain to him what manner of entities were assaulting him at night. I asked him to try a simple protective countermeasure (one of the ones I had shown B.) when he went home. After a few minutes of explanation, he seemed to understand what to do, and we parted company, agreeing I would call him early the next day, before he left for work.

I did a lot of thinking that night. Even though certain elements of his tale did not match other accounts of individual types of psychic attacks, when looked at together, the elements began to make sense in their own way. I formed my own theory as to what was probably happening at S.'s house. You can decide for yourself if you agree or not, based on what happened later.

At first I was uncertain why S. would feel some kind of energy field in his house. When he mentioned the sensation of walking through cobwebs, I began to see that it might indicate some paranormal presence. In many cases of hauntings, and even during controlled seances or channeling sessions, a cobweb sensation indicates that something unseen is nearby. (We won't go into that any further here, but those who are interested can find, with a little occult research, several examples to support the fact.)

I then considered the fact that S. not only felt a presence in his house at certain times of the day, but often felt drained or weak in that same house. Remember, he would feel tired even before the night attacks began, which led me to believe he was possibly being slightly drained of lifeforce during the daytime as well. I had found in the past that daytime attacks were common only in public, where a living vampire could at least see his or her victim. For that reason, I couldn't figure out at first why S. was being attacked during the daytime in the privacy of his own home.

However, I considered that he was also being attacked at night more frequently than had occurred during any other case I had heard before. Then a disturbing idea came to mind. The nighttime attacks of the vampires showed that they were actively feeding at night, and therefore, most likely remaining dormant during the day. If S. was still near them during the day, that could mean that at least one of the vampires was using his house as a resting place!

We already discussed how dead psychic vampires would probably, as a result of occult magnetism, use their mortal remains as a resting place during their inactive hours. That's not to say that a vampire couldn't also choose to rest as a free energy being somewhere else. Also, what if the corpse of a vampire was destroyed? Not everyone is buried; cremation, for example, is an inexpensive alternative. An astral vampire could possibly just pick a place to rest during the day (or whenever its inactive period is). Of course, it is possible that it would be a place it was fond of while still alive, but speculating on that motivation is not really important for our discussion. Let's just assume that at least one such vampire, if not several, chose S.'s house for a lair.

A dead astral vampire can most likely feed without consciously trying. If a vampire's astral form is used to feeding, then whenever the form comes into contact with an energy source, it will probably feed. So it is likely that S. had, on occasion, walked right into or through such a resting vampire, and as a result, was slightly drained by it. We obviously will never know whether or not the vampire was aware of S.'s presence. Perhaps at first it wasn't, which is why it took a few weeks for the nighttime attacks to begin.

Finally, there was the fact that S. was never attacked two nights in a row. It was disturbing to think that the vampires were probably letting him regenerate just enough lifeforce between their feedings so that they would always have a source of sustenance at "home."

Having come to those conclusions, I called S. He answered, sounding a bit groggy, and I wondered for a moment if he had been attacked again. However, I soon learned he had just woken up, and had not had any "visitors" the night before. After talking for a while, I learned that he was attacked the night before I met him. Considering that he was never attacked two nights in a row, I had no assurance that the simple protection ritual I told him to perform would work or had worked. B. had used that only as a preparation for another rite (again, those protections will be explained in the next chapter).

He didn't have much time to talk before going to work, but I managed to explain to him some of the conclusions I had drawn, and told him I would call him in the evening with better preventative measures for him to take. I never expected what happened next.

When I tried calling at around six o'clock that night, I got no answer. S. had told me he would be home by then, but I figured I'd try calling back later. (I chose not to give him my phone number at the fair because of past experiences I had with people who were interested in relating their "stories.")

I called again at about 7:30 P.M., and finally got an answer. It was S., but sounding as I had never heard him. He was whispering and talking rapidly, asking me if I could please meet him at a diner near where he lived. I knew how to get to the one he was talking about, and I decided I'd go—he sounded absolutely frantic.

As I pulled into the parking lot, I could see him waiting in the lobby. When I got inside, I noticed a bruise on his forehead and tried asking him about it, but he said that we should go in and have a seat first.

At the booth, he told me everything. As it turned out, he had gotten home at about 5:30 that evening, and went to rest in his room, waiting for my call. He sat on his bed, and started to read a magazine to pass the time. After what "couldn't have been more than two minutes," he heard a faint "rumbling." At first he thought it might be a truck outside, but S. told me that no matter how much he walked around the room, he couldn't pinpoint which direction it was coming from. It seemed to be surrounding him.

Then, when he turned to leave the room to see if it was just as loud in the other rooms, he felt something heavy slam against his back, sending him head-first into the wall. He didn't pass out, however, and turned around to find that his bed was up against him—standing on its side! Whatever force had driven the bed to hit him had also managed to put two of its four posts into his wall.

I could tell by the look he gave me that there was more, so I waited. I'll never forget what he told me next: "It was still bright in my room, but I saw it. It looked brown, but see-through, and it talked to me.... It used the rumbling to make its words."

I asked him to explain what that sounded like, and he said the rumbling in the room was somehow "shaped" by the creature to create a voice. In the past, I had listened to tapes made of "electronic voice phenomena," where static on a tape seemed to form voices (many believe them to be the voices of the dead, but that's possibly a topic for another book). The thought of this vampire somehow generating a noise and then shaping it amazed me. I asked what it said.

S. told me that the creature issued him a short and some-what cryptic warning: "Never speak again of our communion." After that was "said," the rumbling faded away, as did the brown phantom form on the other side of the bed. S. went out-side to sit on his porch and think. (He apparently just missed my first phone call.) He then went back in to "take care of a few things." I had called as he was just "finishing up." He wouldn't elaborate on what he meant.

I tried to tell him that I had shown him only a preliminary protection rite last night, and that the other techniques I had to show him might be of help, but he wouldn't listen. He had a distant look on his face and basically ignored me for a few moments. I figured I would give him some time to calm down, and just sat drinking my tea. He then got up, and said "I'll be right back."

I watched him head toward the back of the diner, where the restrooms were, and as I was visually following his progress, I saw an old friend of mine. He came over and we talked for a while. After a few minutes, I began to wonder what happened to S. and, excusing myself, went back to the bathroom area. No one was in the men's room, and when I checked the back door, I found it was unlocked. Had S. left that way? And if he had, why?

I asked around, and no one had seen him. When I finally left, I found a note made of toilet paper stuffed under my windshield wiper. It just said, "I took everything with me that matters. I can't go back there again. Thanks for your help. Please don't follow me. S." (He actually signed his full first name.) I never saw him again. His phone was disconnected soon after.

A little research uncovered the fact that his number was unlisted, and finding out where he lived was therefore impossible. I would have appreciated the chance to see the house and maybe look into the case further, but that never came to be. Trying to find out S.'s current whereabouts seemed an invasion of privacy, especially after what his note said, so I haven't pursued the case any further.

Without having actually "seen" any of the incidents in this particular case, I can't vouch for its authenticity. I suppose it could all be a hoax, but I don't feel that it is. Maybe, instead, those six words S. claims he heard in his bedroom had a profound effect on him. The strain that S.'s constant attacks were putting on him must have been dreadful, and I'm not surprised that he ran off to escape his predicament. In his case, where the vampire(s) bothering him might have been living in his house, there is a good chance that running was the answer, for him. But what about the next inhabitants of that or other houses? Just what types of dangers can such vicious psychic vampires pose?

This case presents quite a mystery. However, if the incidents described by S. are true, some intentional psychic vampires might be capable of direct physical harm (i.e. the moving bed), although I haven't seen evidence of other such attacks, and can't say for certain that astral vampires can affect physical things.

I'm pretty certain of one thing, though: From what I have seen, heard, and read, psychic vampires are real. Whether they know of their nature or act unconsciously, they can be dangerous. What they do to survive can seriously harm anyone they feed upon.

Well, almost anyone; there are ways for people to protect themselves. Read on, because in the next chapter, we'll see how that's done.

Chapter Ten

Protection from Psychic Vampires

One natural instinct that all humans share is that of averting danger. In real life, few individuals go out of their way to look for danger—most people naturally seek sanctuary from harm.

While avoiding dangerous situations in the physical world is not always possible, some basic precautions can be taken. Security systems are often installed in high-crime areas, people tend to travel in groups after hours, and so on. In this information age, tips for staying safe can be found in numerous sources.

What about the dangers of the astral plane? As we've seen so far, there might be a need to learn about, and take precautions against, ethereal dangers as well as physical ones. The information on how to do that, however, is not so widely available. This chapter should help change that.

To some, the techniques given here might seem to be "magic." That's for a good reason—they are. Magic can be thought of as an applied science. It comes as no surprise that the procedures used by someone performing a feat of mechanical engineering are simply pragmatic applications of the principles of physics or chemistry. Likewise, the techniques used by someone performing a magical ritual are practical ways of using the knowledge of occult science.

However, for those somewhat uncomfortable with the idea of performing a magical rite (as B. was at first), at least read the descriptions of the techniques before making up your mind. The rituals are for the most part similar to meditations, and can be thought of simply as psychic exercises (when performed properly, magic is basically a controlled use of one's psychic power).

As discussed earlier in the book, some of the basic ideas for the techniques in this chapter were drawn from a number of sources, and through experimentation and modification, were developed into the usable forms given here. Other ideas were generated "from scratch" based on my research. When used together, the simple rites given in this chapter form a powerful system of protection against the attacks of psychic vampires (and any psychic attack, for that matter); this is the first time this particular system of defense has appeared in print.

Due to the testing and refining of the rites, the reader can be assured that they do work. With a bit of effort, someone who performs the techniques should be able to go about his or her life, completely unaffected by psychic vampires.

A Purification

Before you attempt to protect yourself psychically, you must first make sure your aura or astral body is free of any etheric "impurities." As you'll soon see, in an instance where someone is repeatedly attacked by a particular psychic vampire, some of those impurities could represent links to the vampire. However, the process of purification will have little effect on such links. Those will have to be taken care of in different ways (more on this later).

The goal of this simple purification rite is to clear away some of the negativities that we all accumulate throughout the day. Doing this will make it easier to "program" our astral bodies for protection, much like a psychic vampire can program its astral form to feed.

Purifications (as well as many other rites) are easier to perform when you have a physical link to aid in concentration. Therefore, because a purification is in fact a psychic cleansing, it is best done while taking either a bath or a shower. In addition to simplifying the necessary visualizations (as you'll see in a moment), taking a bath or shower, particularly at night, can help one relax, and therefore, enter a naturally altered state of mind conducive to psychic work.

For these reasons, always try to practice this rite before you perform the others. Here it is, step by step.

Prepare a bath and enter it, or get into the shower as you normally do (you might want to try the ritual both ways to see which physical link "feels" right, although if you're short on time, a shower is probably preferable).

Close your eyes and really "feel" the water on your skin. If you're in the shower, concentrate on the tingling sensation caused by the stream of water hitting you. If you're taking a bath, focus on the feeling of being surrounded by liquid.

After about a minute of silent meditation on these sensations, you should be ready to imagine there is more than just liquid pulsing against you or surrounding you. Imagine that the tingling of the shower stream is a static field of energy surrounding you. For those taking a bath, pretend the liquid sensation all around you is an aura of energy.

Keep your eyes closed and try to "astrally see" or visualize what the energy field surrounding you might look like.

When you feel you can somewhat imagine your astral body, begin to look for any dark spots in it. If you don't see any, or are having a difficult time visualizing, just assure yourself that you are aware of your aura and any impurities it might have.

Visualize the dark impurities leaving your aura and either being washed away by the shower stream, or simply being absorbed by the water around you.

When you feel you've "cleansed" yourself as much as you can, carefully but quickly get out of the shower, or get up from the bathtub and step out. Turn off the shower or let the tub drain.

You are now free of many impurities and ready to go on to the next simple, yet effective, rite.

A Banishing Ritual

Just as your astral body must be purified before your workings can be done, so too must the astral atmosphere of the room in which you plan to do your work be cleansed. All impurities and negativities must be banished from the area, and to accomplish that, a banishing ritual should be performed. This type of ritual has another function in addition to clearing an area—it also creates a safe place where astral vampires cannot enter or manifest.

We will be using physical links in this rite also; one of them will be the same physical link as in the purification—water. However, in this ritual it will be used to represent the magical element of Water; there are four other elements: Spirit, Earth, Fire, and Air. In addition to a glass of water, the other items you will need are a dish of salt for Earth, a white candle for Fire, and a stick of incense for Air (frankincense works well, although any scent can be used). The element of Spirit will not be represented physically.

Have these items set up on a small table in the center of your room before you begin your purification bath. That way, when you return to your room, you can immediately perform the banishing.

Position the incense on a holder to the east side of your table, the candle in a holder on the south side, the glass of water on the west, and the dish of salt on the north. Have some matches handy as well.

After your purification bath, enter the room where you will be doing your working, dim the lights, and perform the following steps.

Stand to the west of your table, facing east. Close your eyes and take three slow, deep breaths. Feel the body of energy around you again as you do so.

Open your eyes, pick up the matches, and light the incense stick. Then carry it around the perimeter of your room, moving clockwise, forming a circle of smoke. As you do so, say either out loud or to yourself: "I purify this space with Air." Return to your position behind the table and put the burning incense back in the holder on the east side of the table.

Light the candle with a match. Pick the candle up and walk clockwise around the perimeter of your sacred circle, while saying: "I purify this space with Fire." Then return to your position behind the table, and leaving the candle lit, place it back into its holder at the south side of your table.

Pick up the glass of water and walk clockwise around your circle. As you do so, mark the perimeter of your circle by sprinkling drops of water on the floor with your fingers. While you are walking, say: "I purify this space with Water." Return to your position behind the table and place the glass to the west side of the table.

Now, take the small dish of salt and begin to walk around the circle again, this time dropping pinches of salt around the circle as you do so (you don't need to scatter much of the substance, it is only a symbolic action). While circling, say: "I purify this space with Earth." Once again, return to your place behind the table, and set the dish of salt in its position on the north side of the table.

The next few steps require absolute concentration, so clear your mind as well as you can at this point. Close your eyes again, take three more deep breaths, and turn your face up. "See" in your mind's eye that there is a glowing ball of light directly above you. Try to see it as clearly as you can.

Imagine that with each inhalation you take from this point on, the ball of white light gets closer. Soon it will come down through the top of your head and move to the center of your chest. Really try to see and sense it. The ball of brilliant white light should make you feel as if there is a source of warm energy pulsing within you.

When you are aware of the light within you, and convinced of its existence, begin to imagine that it is getting larger with each exhalation. In about a minute it should become a sphere of light that is large enough to surround you and the table. Keep expanding the sphere of Spirit in your mind until it fills the entire circle you just made with the other elements. You will now be surrounded by a circle/sphere made of all five of the ancient magical elements.

At this point you will have to select a symbol that you feel represents protection. (It can be a cross, Star of David, pentagram, etc.) Once you have that symbol in your mind, try to visualize it (with your eyes closed) as being about the size of your hand and floating inside your chest where the ball of energy was. Imagine it to be glowing a soft golden color.

When you can "see" the symbol in your chest, open your eyes. Now visualize the symbol floating to the east of your circle. This time see it as being about two feet tall and glowing in blue light.

Once you can see the symbol to the east of your circle, turn to face the south and visualize the same symbol floating there.

Go on to visualize the symbol in the same manner in the west and north quarters of your circle/sphere.

Seal the sphere around you by visualizing the symbol flat below you at the edge of the sphere below the ground. Then look up and visualize the symbol flat above you at the top edge of your protective sphere.

Finally, concentrate on the circle and symbols around you and say: "I stand now in sacred space. Only light may enter this purified area."

The preceding banishment will work well to create a psychically protected area. Anyone should be able to perform it successfully, without ever having done magical or meditative work before. If you would like to try some advanced banishing rituals, there are some given in my book *Summoning Spirits* (see the Bibliography for details).

Breaking the Ties

After your banishment, you can leave the candle and incense burning. For the rest of the techniques, you will need to move to a place where you can comfortably sit or lie. If you choose to lie down, however, make sure that you will not fall asleep. Sitting in a comfortable chair is probably the best way to do this rite and the one that follows it.

The purpose of this ritual is to remove any links that a psychic vampire might have established with you. This rite needs to be performed only if you are suffering from repeated vampire attacks. When that occurs, astral tendrils (as described earlier in the book) from the vampire could remain linked to your aura, making it easier for the vampire to find you.

Performing this rite is difficult for those new to meditation, because it requires that you sense these connections. However, even if you're not certain of your ability to find the astral tendrils that might be there, simply visualizing that they are there and dealing with them as shown below will result in the same outcome. In other words, your aura will reject and repel the tendrils regardless of where on your astral body they really are, if you symbolically get rid of them.

Once you are comfortably seated, close your eyes. Take three deep breaths and again try to become aware of the subtle astral body surrounding you.

When you can sense and see your astral body's presence, try to "look" for areas of your aura that seem to feel "wrong." In other words, search for areas that just don't feel the same as the rest of your energy body.

Those areas, if you sense any, might have tendrils connected to them. This is especially the case if you are suffering from repeated psychic attacks. Try to see or sense those dark tendrils. If you can't find any after a few minutes, but do feel that you have areas of your astral body that might be lacking in energy, try to visualize tendrils in those areas anyway (for the reasons of symbolism that we already discussed).

Open your eyes and try to see and sense where the astral tendrils are. Make sure you can tell where they are before moving on to the next step.

Lift your right hand, and extend your pointer finger. Imagine there is a foot-long beam of yellow light emanating from the tip of your finger. Feel it pulsing like a short sword of energy.

Use the light sword to cut the tendrils off your astral body. The dark shapes should writhe away from you. "Burn" the edge of each one with your sword after you cut it loose.

When all the tendrils have been cut away, let your light sword dissipate, and spend a few moments feeling your energy body. Sense that it is sealed off and vibrant.

By visualizing cutting away the dark tendrils, even if you had to imagine that they were there at all, you are performing a powerful act of separation from whatever astral vampire might be connected to you. After completion of the rites described so far, you should be purified, in a sacred area, and free of any links to psychic vampires. Now it's time to make sure that no matter where you are, you will be safe from both future daytime and nighttime attacks.

Astral-Body Programming

Psychic vampires can teach their astral bodies to feed off the energy of others. However, we've also mentioned another type of programming—a way for a person to teach his or her astral body to defend and ward off any attacks. Once your astral body is "set" to protect itself in that way, you will only occasionally have to reinforce its programming to enjoy a lifetime of safety from astral attack.

Of course I haven't been able to test the results of this technique over the course of a lifetime, but it has kept people free of attacks since they've started using it. There's no reason why it should stop working. From what I've seen, performing this rite once a month or so (in conjunction with at least the first two rites) virtually guarantees you will never be bothered by a psychic vampire.

That one-month rule could vary from person to person. For example, if you've been attacked on a regular basis by a psychic vampire in the past, you might want to start by doing the ritual every week for about a month, then switching to every other week for a month, then finally to once a month. Alternatively, if you've been attacked only once or never, but want to be on the safe side, you might feel secure and pleased doing it only every once in a while. How often you should reinforce this rite should be determined by experimentation and your particular situation.

You will not need any physical implements to perform this technique, just a comfortable place to sit—wherever you did the "Breaking the Ties" rite will be fine. If you are performing the last rite before this one, then just take a few deep breaths and go immediately into this rite. If you are doing only a banishing beforehand, sit in your comfortable spot and proceed with the following steps.

With your eyes closed, continue concentrating on your astral body. See it as a body of white light surrounding you, and really concentrate on feeling its presence.

Feel your astral body of light expand with each inhalation and contract with each exhalation; in other words, think of it as a balloon-like layer of etheric skin that is affected by your breathing. Feeling that sensation will help you become aware of your body of light in a more "real" way. Realize you can completely control your astral body's dimensions and motions, and that breathing is only one way of doing so.

When you feel you have your aura under conscious control, continue making it expand with each inhalation. However, do not make that etheric skin contract with your exhalations from this point on. As a result of that steady expansion, your aura will continue to grow each time you breathe in.

The farther your aura gets from your physical skin, the less it will resemble your shape. When the etheric skin reaches a distance of about two feet from your physical skin, the former should resemble a large oval of white light that completely encases you. Stop increasing its size at that point.

Spend about a minute trying to focus on the astral shield surrounding you. Make sure you believe it's there before you continue.

Concentrate on the fact that the shield that now surrounds you cannot be penetrated. Repeat several times a mantra similar to the following one: "I am shielded from all psychic attack; I am protected from all harm." You could say this to yourself or out loud, but either way, make sure you say it with each long, drawn-out exhalation. Repetition in sync with rhythmic breathing will make your intent clear to your subconscious, which will in turn effect the changes to your astral body (we can't get into how it is possible to affect the mental plane here, but several of the books in the Bibliography, including *Summoning Spirits*, should make that clearer). Keep repeating your mantra as you continue.

To further reinforce your affirmation or mantra, visualize your aura growing brighter with each exhalation as you repeat your statement of intent. Do that for about three exhalations, then, with each repetition of the mantra, see astral needles forming on the surface of your aura. Add more needles as you repeat the mantra two more times.

Stop repeating your mantra, and concentrate on the appearance of your enlarged astral body. It should be heavily armored with needles, resembling a porcupine. Spend a moment convincing yourself that is the case.

Still concentrating on your armored aura, repeat the following mantra, or one like it, for your next three exhalations: "These spikes shall repel all harm, by day and night."

On your next exhalation, say with conviction, and in a way that feels different and somewhat more powerful: "When danger is near, these spikes shall appear!"

Now, with each exhalation, begin to see your astral shell decrease in size. As it gets to be only about a foot away from the surface of your skin, see the astral shell beginning to resemble your general shape again. Also, at that distance, imagine the needles decreasing in size.

When your aura has shrunk to the size of your body, see it as once again being smooth, and feel it as a part of your physical being. Meditate for a moment on the fact that from this point on, your astral body will swell and form its protective spikes if you are ever under psychic attack.

Open your eyes and slowly get up. You should now do something to fully return to normal consciousness. Eating, watching television, or going for a walk outside are good things to do.

When you finish and are returning to normal consciousness, do not think about the rite! Let the astral "seed" you planted grow without disturbance. Thinking about the procedure might adversely affect its outcome. Try to distract yourself for at least the rest of that day for best results.

With that rite done, and occasionally reinforced, you should be able to go through life unharmed by psychic attack. If you ever feel uncertain that it is working, however, simply bring back the visualization and feeling of the astral shell with its needles and you should immediately feel a sense of security.

One last word on this particular technique. While the rite might seem a bit bizarre to those who are unfamiliar with ritual work, I'd like to make it absolutely clear that the forces set in motion by its performance are powerful and effective. You don't need to take my word for its effectiveness. Try it and see. If you have been bothered by astral vampires in the past, you will enjoy the days of peace that are ahead of you. And if you haven't been attacked, but still perform the rites in this chapter, rest assured that you'll never have a reason to fear the energy-draining creatures described in this book.

Conclusion

It is 11:00 P.M. With her protective ritual and late-night
snack finished, the girl prepares for sleep. Already in her
nightgown, she only has one thing left to do; using a spoon,
she snuffs out the candle on her night table, and gets into bed.
The atmosphere of her room feels different than normal, but
not in a bad way as it did a few nights ago. Her surroundings
feel... safe.

Sleep comes over her.

Once she stirs in the middle of the night, and half asleep,
she can barely make out some presence outside of her room.
In a second the presence is gone, and she forgets all about it as
her peaceful sleep and dreams overtake her once again.

They might not turn into bats, they might not live forever, and they might not even drink blood, but as we've seen, there just might be such beings as vampires.

The incidents related in these pages, and the theories that accompany them, will most likely raise questions in the minds of all who read this book. Perhaps those who would like to believe that vampires exist will find new explanations to explain the creatures' existence. At the other end of the spectrum, true skeptics might find here a delightful number of occult ideas to refute, one at a time.

All that is fine, of course, but I hope instead that the majority of those who read this occult treatise on vampirism will look at this work in another way: mainly, as one person's research and ideas. No information, especially information having to do with the paranormal, should be accepted blindly. No information should be rejected blindly, either. Information should be analyzed before one's opinions are formed.

Whatever conclusions you might draw, I hope you enjoyed this study of the creatures of the night. Remember, for those with open minds, there are always new discoveries to be made. Even if they are of ancient things...

... such as vampires.

Bibliography

Bardon, Franz. *Initiation into Hermetics*. Wuppertal, West Germany: Dieter Ruggeberg Verlag, 1987.

Barber, Paul. *Vampires, Burial, and Death*. New Haven: Yale University Press, 1988.

Barrett, Francis. *The Magus: A Complete System of Occult Philosophy*. New York: Citadel Press, 1989.

Calmet, Augustine. *The Phantom World*. London: Richard Bentley, 1850 (published as two volumes).

Crowley, Aleister. *Magick*. New York: Samuel Weiser, 1973.

Dresser, Norine. *American Vampires: Fans, Victims, Practitioners*. New York: W. W. Norton and Co., 1989.

Evans-Wenz, W. Y. *The Tibetan Book of the Dead*. New York: Causeway Books, 1973.

Florescu, Radu R., and McNally, Raymond T. *Dracula: Prince of Many Faces: His Life and Times*. Boston: Little, Brown and Company, 1989.

Fortune, Dion. *Psychic Self-Defence: A Study in Occult Pathology and Criminality.* Northamptonshire, England: Aquarian Press, 1988.

Garden, Nancy. *Vampires.* New York: Bantam Skylark, 1973.

Guiley, Rosemary Ellen. *Vampires Among Us.* New York: Pocket Books, 1991.

Hare, Augustine. *Story of My Life.* London: George Allen, 1896-1900 (published in six volumes).

Hoyt, Olga. *Lust for Blood.* New York: Stein and Day, 1984.

Hufford, David J. *The Terror that Comes in the Night: An Experience-Centered Study of Supernatural Assault Traditions.* Philadelphia: University of Pennsylvania Press, 1982.

Judith, Anodea. *Wheels of Life: A User's Guide to the Chakra System.* St. Paul, MN: Llewellyn Publications, 1994.

Konstantinos. *Summoning Spirits: The Art of Magical Evocation.* St. Paul, MN: Llewellyn Publications, 1995.

Kraig, Donald Michael. *Modern Magick: Eleven Lessons in the High Magickal Arts.* St. Paul, MN: Llewellyn Publications, 1989.

Lawson, John. *Modern Greek Folklore and Ancient Greek Religion.* New York: University Books, 1964.

Levi, Eliphas. *Transcendental Magic: Its Doctrine and Ritual.* New York: Samuel Weiser, Inc., 1974.

McNally, Raymond T. *Dracula Was a Woman: In Search of the Blood Countess of Transylvania.* New York: McGraw-Hill, 1983.

Noll, Richard. *Vampires, Werewolves and Demons: Twentieth-Century Reports in the Psychiatric Literature.* New York: Brunner Mazel, 1992.

Summers, Montague. *The Vampire, His Kith and Kin.* London: Routledge and Kegan Paul, 1928.

Thompson, E. Campbell. *The Devils and Evil Spirits of Babylonia*. London: Luzac, 1903-1904 (published in two volumes).

Varma, Devendra P. "The Vampire in Legend, Lore, and Literature." (Introduction to the novel: *Varney the Vampire*. New York: Arco Press, 1970.)

Wright, Dudley. *Vampires and Vampirism*. Scotland: Tynron Press, 1991.

Index

magical elements, 176

magnetism, 61-62, 166

Malaysia, 9, 24

Marduk, 19

mental body, 155

Mesopotamia, 15, 17, 19-20, 22

Mexico, 33

mirrors, 41, 117

mortal blood-drinking
dangers of, 171
motivations, 69, 86, 101

mysticism, 28, 111, 113

Nachtzehrer, 32

Nadilla, 21-22

Newfoundland, 27, 34, 122, 125

nighttime attack, 128, 151, 159

nosferatu, 31

obayifo, 27

occult theories
psychic vampirism, 13, 27, 34,
63, 83, 114, 121, 123, 125, 127,
129, 131, 133, 135-136, 138,
145-146, 150, 153, 157-158
sympathetic magic, 62

Old Hags, 34, 122

*One Thousand and One Arabian
Nights,* 21

Order of the Dragon, 70

paralysis (of victim), 9, 130

penanggalan, 25

phantom-like vampire, 5, 44

Plogojowitz, Peter, 5, 32, 39, 43-
45

Poland, 31

powers (vampiric), 3, 7-10, 14, 62,
96, 108-109, 111, 130, 142-143,
153, 172, 179

primary powers, 8-9

psychic attack, 145, 172, 181-182

psychic energy, 9, 11-12, 19, 27,
125-126, 132-133, 135, 138-
140, 155-156, 159

psychic vampires
intentional, 12-13, 17-18, 27,
61, 121, 127, 130-131, 133-134,
136, 152-153, 155-157, 159-
161, 163, 165, 167, 169
unintentional, 11-12, 61, 121,
127, 130-131, 133, 136-139,
141-143, 145, 147, 149, 151-
152

psychic vampirism, 13, 27, 34, 63,
83, 114, 121, 123, 125, 127,
129, 131, 133, 135-136, 138,
145-146, 150, 153, 157-158

psychometry, 139

purification, 172-175

raksashas, 24

raksashis, 24

Renfield, 11, 86-88

Renfield's Syndrome, 11, 86-87

Rice, Anne, 3, 28, 59, 92

Romania, 30-32

running water, 26, 111

Russia, 31

sacred wafer, 37

Second Death, 154-156, 159-160

secondary powers, 8-9, 14

Seven Demons, 19

shamanism, 113

sharp objects, 116

sounds (heard during nighttime
attacks), 151, 163

South America, 33

Spirits of Babylonia, 18

☽ REACH FOR THE MOON

Llewellyn publishes hundreds of books on your favorite subjects! To get these exciting books, including the ones on the following pages, check your local bookstore or order them directly from Llewellyn.

Order by Phone
- Call toll-free within the U.S. and Canada, 1-877-NEW WRLD
- In Minnesota, call (651) 291-1970
- We accept VISA, MasterCard, and American Express

Order by Mail
- Send the full price of your order (MN residents add 7% sales tax) in U.S. funds, plus postage & handling to:
    Llewellyn Worldwide
    P.O. Box 64383, Dept. 1-56718-380-8
    St. Paul, MN 55164–0383, U.S.A.

Postage & Handling
- **Standard** (U.S., Mexico, & Canada)

If your order is:

$20.00 or under, add $5.00

$20.01–$100.00, add $6.00

Over $100, shipping is free

(Continental U.S. orders ship UPS. AK, HI, PR, & P.O. Boxes ship USPS 1st class. Mex. & Can. ship PMB.)

- **Second Day Air** (Continental U.S. only): $10.00 for one book + $1.00 per each additional book
- **Express** (AK, HI, & PR only) [Not available for P.O. Box delivery. For street address delivery only.]: $15.00 for one book + $1.00 per each additional book
- **International Surface Mail:** Add $1.00 per item
- **International Airmail:** Books—Add the retail price of each item; Non-book items—Add $5.00 per item

Please allow 4–6 weeks for delivery on all orders.
Postage and handling rates subject to change.

Discounts
We offer a 20% discount to group leaders or agents. You must order a minimum of 5 copies of the same book to get our special quantity price.

Free Catalog
Get a free copy of our color catalog, *New Worlds of Mind and Spirit*. Subscribe for just $10.00 in the United States and Canada ($30.00 overseas, airmail). Call 1-877-NEW WRLD today!

Visit our website at www.llewellyn.com for more information.

SUMMONING SPIRITS
The Art of Magical Evocation
by Konstantinos

Evoking spirits is one of the most powerful and beneficial magical techniques you can use. But for centuries, this technique has either been kept secret or revealed in unusable fragments by those with little practical evocation experience. *Summoning Spirits* is a complete training manual, written by a practicing magician. This book makes performing evocations easy to do, even if you've never performed a magical ritual before.

Using the simple instructions in this manual, you can summon spiritual entities to effect miraculous changes in your life. Obtain mystical abilities ... locate hidden "treasure" ... control the weather ... even command a spirit "army" to protect your home while you're away! You will learn how to perform evocations to both the astral and physical planes, plus opening and banishing rituals. Do exercises designed to prepare you for magical workings and astral travel, discover how to create a manufactured spirit, consecrate your magical implements and much more. Includes complete sample rituals.

1-56718-381-6, 240 pgs., 7 x 10, illus., softcover $14.95

NOCTURNAL WITCHCRAFT
Magick After Dark
by Konstantinos

Nightkind, goths, children of the night . . . by whichever name you call them, they represent a major force in the New Age world. They are seekers intrigued by the mysteries of the occult and Witchcraft, yet disappointed by books that equate dark mysteries with evil.
This book delivers a unique experience, beginning with an explanation of why some are drawn to the night and the aspects of deity that represent the dark, followed by powers and rituals available under the cover of shadow. From divining with the night to reading minds, from enhancing personal magnetism to altering reality, *Nocturnal Witchcraft* fulfills the esoteric needs of anyone who appreciates dark mystique.

0-7287-0166-1, 288 pgs., 6 x 9, softcover $14.95

WHEELS OF LIFE
A User's Guide to the Chakra System
by Anodea Judith

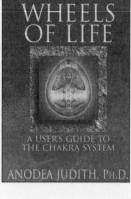

An instruction manual for owning and operating the inner gears that run the machinery of our lives. Written in a practical, down-to-earth style, this fully illustrated book will take the reader on a journey through aspects of consciousness, from the bodily instincts of survival to the processing of deep thoughts.

Discover this metaphysical system under the light of popular Western metaphors: quantum physics, elemental magick, Kabbalah, physical exercises, meditations, and visionary art. This book is a vital resource for magicians, Witches, Pagans, mystics, yoga practitioners, martial arts people, psychologists, medical people, and all those who are concerned with holistic growth techniques.

0-87542-320-5, 544 pgs., 6 x 9, illus., softcover $17.95

PSYCHIC DEVELOPMENT FOR BEGINNERS
An Easy Guide to Releasing and Developing Your Psychic Abilities
by William Hewitt

Psychic Development for Beginners provides detailed instruction on developing your sixth sense, or psychic ability. Innovative exercises like "The Skyscraper" allow beginning students of psychic development to quickly realize personal and material gain through their own natural talent.

Benefits range from the practical to spiritual. Find a parking space anywhere, handle a difficult salesperson, choose a compatible partner, and even access different time periods! Practice psychic healing on pets or humans—and be pleasantly surprised by your results. Use psychic commands to prevent dozing while driving. Preview out-of-body travel, cosmic consciousness and other alternative realities. Instruction in *Psychic Development for Beginners* is supported by personal anecdotes, 44 psychic development exercises, and 28 related psychic case studies to help students gain a comprehensive understanding of the psychic realm.

1-56718-360-3, 216 pgs., 5¼ x 8, softcover $9.95

CONTACT THE OTHER SIDE
7 Methods for Afterlife Communication
Konstantinos

Are you ready to make contact with loved ones on the other side? One of the nation's foremost vampire experts now turns his talents to the age-old quest for communication with the dead. This is the first book in the modern marketplace to focus on practical, usable techniques for communicating with spirits.

Whether you've been frustrated in the past by afterlife books that cite case studies but no usable methods, or are just now entering the world of paranormal communication, your search for proof is over. You don't have to be an electronics whiz or master of a secret occult discipline to capture the voices and images of the dead on audio and video tape, or to communicate with them via your mind alone. This book will guide you to the most awe-inspiring experiences you'll ever have while still alive—to your own contact with deceased loved ones and other souls.

Speak with them. They're waiting.

0-87542-377-8, 240 pgs., 6 x 9, bibliog., index $14.95

PSYCHIC EMPOWERMENT
A 7-Day Plan for Self-Development
Joe Slate, Ph.D.

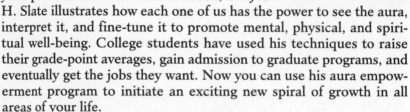

Imagine an advanced energy/information system that contains the chronicle of your life—past, present, and future. By referring to it, you could discover exciting new dimensions to your existence. You could uncover important resources for new insights, growth, and power.

You possess such a system right now. It is your personal aura. In his latest book, Dr. Joe H. Slate illustrates how each one of us has the power to see the aura, interpret it, and fine-tune it to promote mental, physical, and spiritual well-being. College students have used his techniques to raise their grade-point averages, gain admission to graduate programs, and eventually get the jobs they want. Now you can use his aura empowerment program to initiate an exciting new spiral of growth in all areas of your life.

1-56718-637-8, 288 pgs., 6 x 9, softcover $12.95

To Order, Call 1-800-THE MOON
prices subject to change without notice